A Love We Don't Deserve

Other Books by Robert Snitko

*Lessons Learned from Jonah: Meditations
on God's Restoring Grace*

*God is Not Black-and-White: Seeking Unity
in a Theologically Diverse Church*

A Love We Don't Deserve

Finding Freedom in God's Grace

By Robert Snitko

WIPF & STOCK · Eugene, Oregon

A LOVE WE DON'T DESERVE
Finding Freedom in God's Grace

Wipf & Stock
An Imprint of Wipf and Stock Publishers
199 W. 8th Ave., Suite 3
Eugene, OR 97401

www.wipfandstock.com

PAPERBACK ISBN: 978-1-5326-9555-1
HARDCOVER ISBN: 978-1-5326-9556-8
EBOOK ISBN: 978-1-5326-9557-5

Scripture taken from THE HOLY BIBLE, NEW INTERNATIONAL VER-
SION®, NIV® Copyright © 1973, 1978, 1984, 2011 by Biblica, Inc.® Used by
permission. All rights reserved worldwide.

Italics in Scripture quotations have been added by the author for emphasis.

Manufactured in the U.S.A.   04/02/20

For all who feel unworthy of God's love.

Contents

Preface

Grace and forgiveness. These seemingly ordinary words have extraordinary implications. The question is: *do we truly understand the weight of these words?* What appear to be two words that are used semi-frequently are actually *actions* that can change our lives. I would suggest that grace and forgiveness are enough for humanity to experience joy, peace, and freedom. If we drink deeply from the cup of grace, we will encounter true forgiveness. As we encounter true forgiveness, we will experience everlasting joy, everlasting peace, and everlasting freedom. I ask the question again: *do we truly understand the weight of these words?* Jesus does.

Jesus was on a mission of bringing reconciliation into a broken—sin-ridden—world. Not only that, but Jesus was seeking to demonstrate the love of God to all who would listen. Jesus would go on to demonstrate the most scandalous act of love for all mankind. He freely surrendered his life for the sake of saving humanity from their sin. It wasn't easy. He wrestled with God—ultimately trusting in God's plan for him.

Jesus freely gives humanity the gift of grace. This gift of grace is his life. Jesus has given his life to all sinners so that they may be made new in him. This grace is nothing that humanity has earned. This grace is certainly not something that humanity has deserved. Yet, Christ, in his unending love towards us, chose to offer it nonetheless. He has chosen to look at brokenness and make it whole. He has chosen to freely offer his life as a means of forgiveness—for the sins of all. Nothing that we have done, are doing, or will do can change the work of Christ on the cross. It is finished.

Grace and *forgiveness.* Do we truly understand the weight of these words? It took one man's life to express the true meaning of these words. It took one man's life to demonstrate how to offer grace to many. It took one man's life to offer the kind of forgiveness that no one else could offer. Join me on this journey as we use Psalm 32 as a platform in finding forgiveness in God's grace. I hope that as you work through these pages, you will find freedom. As you work through this book, questions for reflection will be provided at the end of each chapter. Once you work through these questions, there will be a space that you can use for journaling and your own reflection. I pray that God will use this resource to excite you in your faith journey while giving you the hope in the gospel of Christ Jesus. I hope that you realize that you don't need to figure everything out in your life in order to experience God's grace and forgiveness; rather that you may come as you are. May you be blessed.

Acknowledgments

There have been many who have influenced and inspired my writing journey for this book. When the Lord put it on my heart to write a book on grace, I could only think about those in my life who have demonstrated what grace looks like.

I'm particularly grateful for my wife, Mags, who is constantly patient with me as I write and who voluntarily allows me to talk my face off as I process my thoughts and ideas with her. Without her grace and support, I wouldn't be able to spend the time writing and getting this book through the finish line. I am forever grateful.

I would also like to express my gratitude to my good friend and ministry partner, Alex Wickell, who leads, challenges, and inspires my ministry. Your graciousness and inspiration propels me to pursue the gifts that the Lord has provided.

My church home, The Branch Community Church in Chicago: this place is filled with grace and love. It is an absolute joy to serve alongside this body of believers. Praise the Lord for the staff, families, and individuals who demonstrate Christlike love each week.

I would like to thank my publisher, Wipf and Stock, for our continued partnership. It is by your grace that I have been given a voice and an opportunity to express my thoughts, passions, and desires through the writing platform.

Finally, I would like to acknowledge my copy editor, Emily Callihan. Thank you for helping me get this book through the finish line.

Introduction

L ife is filled with fiery trials that test our character as people. There is no doubt that ups and downs will come our way—the question is: how will we handle those times? Perhaps you've committed a sin that is weighing you down to the point of being lost, unable to find forgiveness. Perhaps you've been working through a trial in your life that has convinced you that God is not good enough. Maybe you're constantly trying to do the right thing, and falling short is torturing you. Or if you're like me, you simply cannot wrap your mind around a God who is so loving and kind that, regardless of your circumstances, he forgives you and has a profound plan for you. God is so good and gracious. His forgiveness is unlike any earthly forgiveness. No matter how much we may have hurt God, he is faithfully seeking a relationship with us. He pursues us. He admires us. He blesses us. He forgives us, by way of his unending grace.

Recently, I have experienced a deep feeling of condemnation for all of the sin that I had previously committed. I began to second-guess the forgiveness of God for all the wrong I have done. I questioned, "Does God actually forgive all people for their rebellion, hatred, and self-infatuation?" That seems ludicrous. I couldn't help but believe in the lies that I am unworthy, invaluable, and undeserving of God's forgiveness and grace. Though I am not worthy (apart from Christ) God, in his grace, is greater than I can imagine. He is not interested in perfect people, or people who have it all together. Rather, he is interested in brokenness. This was difficult for me to believe even though I knew the truth. I felt like a wretch. Unworthy of forgiveness. As I was longing to hear from God, I flipped through the pages of Scripture, hoping to hear and discover truth even though I was believing lies about who God is.

God met me. He spoke to me. My eyes began to sweat (as my wife would say). I couldn't believe in the words I was reading—yet I believed. God's word spoke to me through David. It touched my heart. I experienced true forgiveness and couldn't help but worship God for it. I found myself reading, rereading, and praying over Psalm 32. It was beautiful. The psalm says,

> Blessed is the one
>> whose transgressions are forgiven,
>> whose sins are covered.
> Blessed is the one
>> whose sin the Lord does not count against them
>> and in whose spirit is no deceit.
>
> When I kept silent,
>> my bones wasted away
>> through my groaning all day long.
> For day and night
>> your hand was heavy on me;
> my strength was sapped
>> as in the heat of summer.
>
> Then I acknowledged my sin to you
>> and did not cover up my iniquity.
> I said, "I will confess
>> my transgressions to the Lord."
> And you forgave
>> the guilt of my sin.
>
> Therefore let all the faithful pray to you
>> while you may be found;
> surely the rising of the mighty waters
>> will not reach them.
> You are my hiding place;
>> you will protect me from trouble
>> and surround me with songs of deliverance.

I will instruct you and teach you in the way you should go;
　　I will counsel you with my loving eye on you.
Do not be like the horse or the mule,
　　which have no understanding
but must be controlled by bit and bridle
　　or they will not come to you.
Many are the woes of the wicked,
　　but the Lord's unfailing love
　　surrounds the one who trusts in him.

Rejoice in the Lord and be glad, you righteous;
　　sing, all you who are upright in heart!

Praise be to our good God for this truth! We are forgiven. The weight of our sin can really trample us, making us feel dead. But God is not interested in us being ruled by sin. God is committed to the pursuit of reconciliation and restoration as he sets us free from the chains that prevent us from experiencing the freedom of his mighty grace. My prayer is that this book helps you see the goodness of God through Psalm 32, even though you may feel unworthy, broken, callused, guilty, bound to sin, hopeless, hurt, shattered, and unloved. In these pages, you will find God's forgiveness by way of his grace. You will find that God does not hold a grudge against you. If he did, he wouldn't have been interested in redeeming all of humanity through the person and work of his Son, Jesus Christ. God is interested in you. He is interested in a growing and personal relationship with you. He wants to meet your every need.

Part One

Unworthy

Chapter 1 | Forgiveness Found in God's Grace

*Blessed is the one whose transgressions are
forgiven, whose sins are covered.*

—Psalm 32:1

W hen I was a young boy, I absolutely loved the Christmas
season. I loved the music, the decorations, the eggnog, and
the Christmas movie marathons on TV. I loved Christmas because Santa would bring me gifts and place them underneath the
Christmas tree. I would wake up on the morning of the twenty-fifth
of December, searching for the labels that read my name. I could tell
Santa was my friend because he would give me lots of gifts. The irony
was that I had never met this Santa character—so he must've seen
some good in me to bring me gifts that I didn't deserve. Looking
back, I wished it could be Christmas every month! Who could say
no to free gifts—even when they're undeserved?

There are many things in this world that we do not deserve.
When we receive gifts from others or are served by others, we often
say that we're "blessed." This word *blessed* can often be interpreted
as being filled with joy, or feeling gratitude. It's not easy to feel
blessed when circumstances in life forbid us from experiencing
true joy, though. The thing that robs us from joy the most is sin.
Sin can be an action, a thought, or a feeling which brings separation between God and mankind. It is our way of wronging God.
The birth of sin occurred in the garden of Eden, after God created
man and woman to enjoy all of creation—and, more importantly,
to enjoy the goodness of God. But mankind was tempted by Satan to partake and eat from the tree that God said not to eat from

(Gen 3:1). This temptation arose as Satan made it more appealing to desire sin. Shortly after the temptation increased, Adam and Eve partook of the tree and consumed its fruit—the forbidden fruit. Immediately they felt guilt and shame befall them (Gen 3:7–10). They knew that they had wronged God, giving birth to sin. Since then, all of mankind is born into the sin of our ancestors. There is no way to hide from it anymore. It exists and it is potent. Due to sin, humanity has severed its relationship with God almighty—causing separation and condemnation. The apostle Paul writes in Romans that "all have sinned and fall short of the glory of God" (Rom 3:23). We are divided from the Creator who made us in his image. We cannot measure up to his goodness and what he requires of us, namely perfection. The problem is that this cannot be attained on our own doing. Humanity is imperfect and broken, unable to right the wrongs of sin. However, God is merciful, just, and gracious enough to have a plan of redemption for all of humanity. This plan involves a free gift that is undeserved.

Forgiveness in Grace

The opening verse in Psalm 32 sets the tone for the rest of the psalm. It functions as the thesis statement of the psalm. David gives us wise insight on experiencing true forgiveness. He extols what it looks like to experience the blessing of forgiveness. David writes, "Blessed is the one whose transgressions are forgiven, whose sins are covered" (Ps 32:1). Oh how happy must one be when they experience the forgiveness of sin. We cannot atone for our own sin, but our sin is indeed covered. It is covered by God's Son, Jesus Christ, the Savior. Jesus is God's plan of redemption for humanity. Jesus entered into the world sinless and blameless. He lived a perfect life on behalf of mankind. Jesus voluntarily gave up his life on the cross at Calvary so that people could experience grace and forgiveness for their sin. He was hurt, beaten, and tortured for the sin of the world (Mark 15:16–32). He went through excruciating pain so that God's creation could have a second chance in life. In fact, because of the cross, we are forgiven over and over again.

There is no limit to the work Christ accomplished on the cross. God's grace is never-ending. God's grace is persistent in chasing after us—even when we run.

Christ Jesus is God's free gift and direct action of saying, "I love you." Regardless of our past, our present, or our future, God loves everyone. His desire is to meet us exactly where we're at, no matter the trial, pain, or difficulty. God meets us in our circumstances, offering us forgiveness for everything that we have ever done to hurt or reject him. This is forgiving grace.

Every single person is guilty of sinning against God and in need of forgiveness. God desires to have a relationship with a broken people who rejected him, as he seeks restoration with them. He longs to be in a perfect union with humanity. This perfection is unattainable by humanity. We have an excessive amount of sin that saturates our lives each day—too much to comprehend. Our thoughts, our desires, our words, our actions, and our hearts all contribute to our inclination to sin. We often desire to atone for our own sin, but this task is impossible. It is impossible to atone for our own sin because we simply cannot. We cannot give an account for each sin we commit due to our tendency to forget a large portion of those sin habits. The forgiveness of sin is not contingent on ourselves as this suppresses the grace of God. There is far more to forgive than we may comprehend. The depth of our sin is insurmountable—thus, it is impossible to please a holy and perfect God. Praise be to God for allowing us to experience the greatest love story ever told. This love story is unlike any other. The sacrificial, personal, and profound nature of this kind of love is beautiful, rich, and filled with grace—a grace that seems to only be available for those who are worthy of receiving it. But the paradox is in the fact that this grace is available for all—especially the unworthy. What kind of love would forgive, heal, redeem, bless, and pursue someone in the midst of their recurring desire for rebellion? This love is breathtaking and it includes the personal and active work of Christ in us—the hope of glory. John writes about this breathtaking love by telling us,

> For God so loved the world that he gave his one and
> only Son, that whoever believes in him shall not perish
> but have eternal life. For God did not send his Son into
> the world to condemn the world, but to save the world
> through him. (John 3:16–17)

Putting our faith and trust in Jesus gives us hope to not perish, but to participate in an eternal relationship with the living Son of God. God's love for humanity is displayed in the sending of Christ, the Savior of the world. Reconciliation is found in our Savior's selfless act of shedding his blood on the cross for our sin. Placing our trust in Christ changes us completely. Through Christ, we're able to comprehend and experience forgiveness at the highest cost.

For the Love of God

"For the love of God" is an often-used idiom that expresses irritation, annoyance, frustration, or exasperation in someone's circumstance. When mulling over this phrase, I can't help but think . . . *does this expression imply that we subconsciously feel this way about God and his love towards us and others?* Do we think that God is irritated, annoyed, frustrated, and is absolutely exasperated with us—his creation? Perhaps. Perhaps God is in the clouds shaking his head and pointing his finger at us because he is an angry God. Perhaps God is extremely unhappy about the way we mistreat people, so he takes note and remembers not to think about us anymore. Perhaps a particular sin in our life has been eating away at us and God can't take it anymore. Because these things exist we think that God can't possibly love us. Naturally we formulate phrases that suggest or imply that we are irritated and annoyed with someone or something, therefore using God's name—particularly the attribute of his love—as a way to emphasize that we are upset. There is a deep, negative connotation that is associated with this idiom, which could harm our approach and perspective of God's love.

So do we have it all wrong in assuming and using the phrase *for the love of God*? Is God actually angry at everyone all the time, thus causing us to associate this idiom with our own frustration? Yes and no. God's wrath is not intended towards us directly. Although, sin is a byproduct of the fall of humanity (Gen 3). Because we embody sin at birth, we experience both the weight of sin and the wrath of God towards sin. However, a wrath-filled God (as we may assume) would not grant a way out if it weren't for his love.

The love of God in Christ gives us deeper insight into David's writing of Psalm 32:1, which ultimately helps us understand the depths of God's forgiveness for humanity. "Blessed is the one whose transgressions are forgiven, whose sins are covered" (Ps 32:1). Divine grace is extended to those who are forgiven for their rebellion and wrongdoing against God and others. Acknowledging our transgressions and putting our faith in Christ covers our sin while setting us free from the chains of death. This is the direct result of the grace of God towards mankind. God's grace allows us to experience true joy and victory over sin and death through his unconditional love for us. This can only occur because God, in his very nature, is love. In John's first epistle, he demonstrates a beautiful reality of God's love:

> This is how God showed his love among us: He sent his one and only Son into the world that we might live through him. This is love: not that we loved God, but that he loved us and sent his Son as an atoning sacrifice for our sins. (1 John 4:9–10)

God demonstrated his very love among us by sending Christ Jesus into the world, so that we might live through him. We can only understand the love of God by understanding the atoning work that Christ completed on the cross for us. Love in itself is not something that humanity can understand and embrace apart from God. German theologian Dietrich Bonhoeffer explains this in his work on ethics:

> God Himself is love. Only he who knows God knows what love is; it is not the other way round; it is not that we first

of all by nature know what love is and therefore know also what God is. No one knows God unless God reveals Himself to him. And so no one knows what love is except in the self-revelation of God. Love, then, is the revelation of God. And the revelation of God is Jesus Christ.[1]

He continues:

God's revelation in Jesus Christ, God's revelation of His love, precedes all our love towards Him. Love has its origin not in us but in God. Love is not an attitude of men but an attitude of God.[2]

Bonhoeffer emphasizes that apart from knowing God, we do not know love. The love of God is expressed through the person and work of Christ. Jesus sacrificed everything for us. His primary goal was to fulfill the will of God. God willed that Jesus would live his life to lose it. This deed was necessary in order to mend rebellious humanity back into a spirit-filled relationship with the Creator of the universe. Why would God be interested in people who naturally choose to drift away from him as they pursue the desire of self? The answer is grace. The grace of God is unending towards his precious creation.

The apostle Paul experienced this firsthand as he wrote his letter to the Romans. In chapter 5 of Romans, Paul addresses the theology of reconciliation. Paul writes, "God demonstrates his own love for us in this: While we were still sinners, Christ died for us" (Rom 5:8). God loves sinners. God in his grace embodied humanity in the form of Jesus Christ—living a perfect and obedient life because we could not do so. Through Christ, who alone has the power to conquer sin by way of atonement on the cross, God brought restoration to the world. This is grace. This is love.

Commentator Leslie C. Allen writes in *The New International Bible Commentary*:

The extent of God's love is shown in that there was nothing admirable or lovely about man which could have

1. Bonhoeffer, *Ethics*, 53.
2. Bonhoeffer, *Ethics*, 53.

evoked it. Human self-sacrifice demands intrinsic worth in its object, whether scrupulous fairness or kindly goodness. God's love, revealed in Christ's death, wonderfully makes no prior demands at all. God has proved how well He loves us, His love is confirmed and enhanced in that it was shown to weaklings, to impious sinners, when He broke into history at the crucial moment, His appointed time for inaugurating a new era of grace.[3]

There is nothing that we can offer to God for him to consider and love us. As Allen notes, there are no prior demands necessary for us to get God's attention. There is no obligation that we must first fulfill in order for God to take notice of us. He takes notice of us because his very nature is love. His love for us was revealed in what took place in the narrative of Jesus' birth, life, death, resurrection, and ascension. Love was displayed on the cross. God saw the wickedness of humanity and wanted to bring about redemption. In his paradoxical love, God allowed his one and only Son—Jesus Christ—to bleed out on the cross, so that salvation might invade the hearts of many. This is good news and we can rejoice in it! Praise be to God for considering us as worthy people, though naturally unworthy. Praise be to God for not forcing us to the cross to pay the penalty of our own sin, but for humbly offering his life—in Christ—in order to unite us with him by way of an eternal relationship. So what is our response to this good news? Our response is to acknowledge that there is nothing that we can do to save ourselves from sin, even though at times we may like to think that we can. The forgiveness of our sin rests solely in the grace of God. A relationship with God is offered to all who would humble themselves enough to say, "I surrender," that we may acknowledge that we are weak and Christ Jesus is our strength. He alone can provide all that we need. He alone is our hope, our comfort, and our peace. Let us humbly lean into Christ and receive his beautiful gift of grace and mercy—that is the gospel, the very person of Christ, who sacrificially laid down his life for us—so that we may have life everlasting.

3. Allen, "Romans," 1325.

The Hope

It can be a difficult thing to accept forgiveness for what we've done. We may feel like we need to make things right. It may feel like we have let someone down so much that nothing can be done to move forward. And it can especially feel like our past, present, and future baggage weighs too much for God to forgive us and set us free. But this couldn't be further from the truth.

Regardless of the selfish, sin-filled brokenness that we have participated in—or continue to participate in—God in his sovereign grace and mercy is faithful to forgive the unworthy. This demonstrates the *perfect* love of God for those who trust in him. This gift of love can be received by all who are willing to embrace the gospel of Christ Jesus. In our acceptance of this gift we are exposed to a love so beautiful; a Father so faithful; a Savior so willing; a Spirit so persistent; a hope never-ending; a grace unchanging; a gift so free.

Questions for Reflection

1. What is the most difficult thing about receiving the free gift of grace?

2. What roadblocks do you face when trying to experience Christ's forgiveness for you?

3. How can you move forward, knowing that God—in his grace—forgives your sin, no matter the depth of your darkness?

4. How can you offer this same kind of grace and forgiveness to others, in light of how you understand Christ's forgiveness for you?

Reflections on Chapter 1 |
Forgiveness Found in God's Grace

*"God in his sovereign grace and mercy
is faithful to forgive the unworthy."*

Chapter 2 | The Atonement of a Savior

Blessed is the one whose sin does not count against
them and in whose spirit is no deceit.

—PSALM 32:2

F ollowing the rules can be an easy task—for some. But for others, it can seem unattainable. For instance, when I cruise in my car, there are these things called "speed limits" and I don't like to agree with them. Living in my neighborhood, it is difficult to speed, though. There are speed traps everywhere. If you exceed the speed limit by five miles per hour, a photo will be taken of your vehicle and license plate number. The city will then send you a wonderful letter in the mail, asking you to pay a fine for speeding. Oh, and of course they have proof with a nice picture they send you of your car caught in the act of speeding. Sometimes I feel like I could be on the cover of the newest car-speedster magazine. But that's just wishful thinking. There are times that the speed trap captures me in the act of speeding, and then sends me a warning because I was close to getting caught in the act—yet I was able to hold my ground. I get a big feeling of relief during these times, taking a deep breath, thanking God for protecting me. See, regardless of it being a warning or a fine, I am breaking the law. And in breaking the law, naturally, I deserve to pay the penalty for my wrongdoing.

We are all law-breakers, whether that be in life, or in the context of God's expectations for us. When Moses led the people of Israel from slavery in Egypt (see Exodus), God sent him the list of Ten Commandments to abide by. Moses was to let Israel know about these commands so that they could serve the one true God. God wanted Israel to have some rules to govern their lives. Israel was disinterested. They were more interested in worshiping a golden calf that seemed a little more appealing. The golden calf was aesthetically pleasing to the eye and many found great value in worshiping the golden calf. Not only that, but the people of Israel were having trouble following the law (Ten Commandments) in general. When we survey the list, the commands are no easy task. Here are the expectations God sent to Moses for the people of Israel:

"I am the Lord your God, who brought you out of Egypt, out of the land of slavery.

"You shall have no other gods before me.

"You shall not make for yourself an image in the form of anything in heaven above or on the earth beneath or in the waters below. You shall not bow down to them or worship them; for I, the Lord your God, am a jealous God, punishing the children for the sin of the parents to the third and fourth generation of those who hate me, but showing love to a thousand generations of those who love me and keep my commandments.

"You shall not misuse the name of the Lord your God, for the Lord will not hold anyone guiltless who misuses his name.

"Remember the Sabbath day by keeping it holy. Six days you shall labor and do all your work, but the seventh day is a sabbath to the Lord your God. On it you shall not do any work, neither you, nor your son or daughter, nor your male or female servant, nor your animals, nor any foreigner residing in your towns. For in six days the Lord made the heavens and the earth, the sea, and all that is in them, but he rested on the seventh day. Therefore the Lord blessed the Sabbath day and made it holy.

"Honor your father and your mother, so that you may live long in the land the Lord your God is giving you.

"You shall not murder.

"You shall not commit adultery.

"You shall not steal.

"You shall not give false testimony against your neighbor.

"You shall not covet your neighbor's house. You shall not covet your neighbor's wife, or his male or female servant, his ox or donkey, or anything that belongs to your neighbor." (Exod 20:2–17)

These are some dense expectations from God that are often seen as impossible to achieve. This is because they are impossible to achieve and to live out faithfully each day. This presents a problem for us: if God expects us to follow these rules, yet we can't, are we doomed? The answer is no. And the reason is Jesus Christ.

The Law

The law provides the standard of living for all. This is why God established the law to the people of Israel (see Exodus). God wanted nothing more than for his people to follow his commands because they had a tendency to forsake him. God is jealous and pursues his people passionately. He longs to have a relationship with his creation, yet his creation repeatedly turns its back on him. God in his faithfulness relentlessly pursues us so that he can forgive us in Christ Jesus, cleansing our sin as we are made white as snow. The law shows us that we are helpless and unable to save ourselves. We are in desperate need of a Savior who will provide a way out of our sin and brokenness. We have the tendency to separate ourselves from the living God as we drift away into our own desires—putting God on the back burner. Yet God in his faithful mercy towards us provides a way of reconciliation. This way is Jesus Christ himself. Due to the work of Christ on our behalf, our sin does not count against us. This is what David is articulating in Psalm 32:2.

David writes, "Blessed is the one whose sin does not count against them and in whose spirit is no deceit" (Ps 32:2). This passage emphasizes David's experience of guilt due to breaking the commands of God. David is aware that God in his goodness reconciles himself to his people, regardless of whether they deserve it or not. Much joy may be found in the realization of God's unending love that is offered to sinners. This unending love does not count sin against a person when their sin is surrendered. God desires his people to be made clean from their sin, so that they may encounter him more personally. We do not need to live under the rule and bondage of sin. Blessed are those who've been freed from sin. Oh how happy is the one whose sin does not count against them!

David is rejoicing in the truth of God's love for his people. God's intention is to redeem a severed relationship with us. Even when there is a list of rules or laws to follow, God is not measuring us according to the these things. In God offering his one and only Son, Jesus Christ, we are able to receive Christ's redemption for our sins—regardless of the law that exists. Our sin is covered by the blood of Christ Jesus and there is nothing that we can do to lose this ardent act of love. God chases us because he loves us, not because we did something to deserve his approval. Being a rule-follower and a law abiding citizen is not going to accomplish victory over our sin. We cannot simply act *rightly* before God and have all our troubles magically disappear. This is because we cannot atone for our actions. What we *do* and *don't do* is not what is at stake when it comes to our justification before a holy God.

Justification by Faith

Historically, followers of God were urged to keep the commandments, as this would prove to God that his people were faithful to him. It didn't take long for all to realize that the commandments were not that easy to follow. If the entirety of the law was followed faithfully, God would be pleased. Humanity quickly proved to God that the law could not be obeyed because of humanity's issue with sin. Therefore, regardless of humanity's tireless effort to abide by the law, absolute obedience could not be accomplished. And if the law of God could not be followed, how could restoration between God and mankind occur? The expectation of one's perfection seems like too much to ask for in an imperfect world. The solution? God, in his mercy and grace, does not expect imperfect creatures to display and perform perfect acts of love towards him and others. We simply cannot obey these standards of the law. So how can we be made right before a holy God and receive justification, all while sustaining the job description of *sinner*? By faith. French theologian John Calvin explains:

> I trust I have now sufficiently shown how man's only re-
> source for escaping from the curse of the law, and recov-
> ering salvation, lies in faith; and also what the nature of
> faith is, what the benefits which it confers, and the fruits
> which it produces. The whole may be thus summed up:
> Christ given to us by the kindness of God is apprehended
> and possessed by faith, by means of which we obtain in
> particular a twofold benefit; first, being reconciled by
> the righteousness of Christ, God becomes, instead of a
> judge, an indulgent Father; and, secondly, being sancti-
> fied by his Spirit, we aspire to integrity and purity of life.[1]

We must be keepers of the law so that we imperfect people may have access to a perfect God. Evidently enough, we are unable to be perfect law-keepers. This is why our faith in Christ is essential. We cannot earn salvation based on the way that we follow the law. We cannot earn salvation based on being a *good* person. We can only earn salvation by putting our faith and trust in what Jesus Christ has done. Praise be to God alone for giving us direct access to his holy throne. The throne of God can only be accessed by the blood of Jesus. Through the blood of Christ we are set free from the law and are justified to the Creator of the universe. In order for us to receive justification we must, by faith, turn to God in repentance, acknowledging our need of his Son, Jesus Christ. It is only through the powerful, atoning work of Christ that we are made one with God. In Christ, our sin does not count against us. We are freed from it. We are forgiven.

Atonement

This word, *atonement*, is profound. Not because the word in and of itself is profound; rather, what it implies in the personhood and

1. Calvin, *Institutes*, 475.

actions of Christ has changed the course of human history. An act of atonement suggests that one desires to offer and preserve reconciliation in this world and in relationships. Though from a humanistic perspective, nothing can cure the harm that has been done in this world. The harm that has been done will always remain. Injustice will always remain. Sin will ultimately always remain a reality. This of course is only true if there is no one to bring about reconciliation to a broken world.

Atonement correlates with the concept of sacrifice. When someone is guilty of wrongdoing, an atonement needs to occur in order to cover the offense. As we surveyed the law that God sent to his people, it is critical to note that the commands are unattainable by a broken and imperfect people. Look back throughout the course of your life in light of the law that God gave the Israelites (the Ten Commandments). Were you able to consistently keep those commands? I know that I was not. It's impossible! We are not capable of perfecting the law. What we are capable of is breaking the law each day. Yet God created the law as a standard of living. So how can we have a relationship with God when we cannot keep the law that he gave us? We have offended God in our disobedience and lack of faithfulness towards him. This makes us guilty before a holy God, and for some a feeling of hopelessness arises because of this. Without the shedding of blood there is no forgiveness of sin (Heb 9:22). Consequently, an atoning sacrifice must take place in order for humanity to experience true freedom from the bondage of sin. This atoning sacrifice must be a perfect, spotless, and blameless sacrifice. Since no being can be perfect in completing this work, Christ Jesus is the glorious solution. God incarnate entered into our humanity to live a perfect life, to then sacrifice himself on the cross so that humanity may be forgiven for their sin. In submission to God's will, Jesus took upon himself the pain of death conquering our sin forevermore. Therefore, we should be filled with joy—absolute joy—for the reality that our sins are forgiven because of a Savior who so graciously gave his life for us.

God's Wrath

So does the solution of Christ's atonement satisfy the wrath of God? Absolutely. God is broken for all of the brokenness that exists. God hurts as he sees his precious creation suffer. And God certainly despises sin because it contradicts his intentions. For some, the issues that exist in this world resemble a wrathful God. God is just in his wrath. But God is also just in his love. This is why the atonement of Jesus Christ was necessary. The wrath of God has been satisfied on the cross of Christ. This means that Jesus Christ perfectly fulfilled the law, living a life that was pleasing to God. There is freedom and power in the name of Jesus. There is freedom in the person of Jesus. There is freedom from the wrath of God in Jesus. Let us taste and see that the Lord is good.

Questions for Reflection

1. Why does the notion of legalism make us feel like we can never be *good* enough?

2. How does our attempt of rule-following hinder our relationship with God?

3. How can you move from legalism to grace?

4. What practical steps can you take to offer grace?

5. What does it mean to you that God's wrath is fully satisfied in Christ?

6. Is your guilt related to the consequences that come with it? In other words, a warning leads us to revisit our sin, whereas a severe consequence may lead us flee.

Reflections on Chapter 2 | **The Atonement of a Savior**

> *"The wrath of God has been satisfied
> on the cross of Christ."*

Chapter 3 | Sin Surrendered

When I kept silent, my bones wasted away
through my groaning all day long. For day and
night your hand was heavy on me; my strength
was sapped as in the heat of summer.

—PSALM 32:3–4

I f you've lived in a warm climate, you know that it can get so hot that you just want to sit indoors all day. Living in Chicago, the weather tends to lean toward the bipolar spectrum. You can experience all four seasons within a day or so (and I'm not making that up, trust me; I've experienced this). Winters are extremely cold and summers are just annoying. It can get pretty hot in Chicago, but not as bad as the time I went to Juarez, Mexico. My church went on a missions trip to build houses in Juarez—a city in Mexico that has undergone much violence and scrutiny. Upon arrival, I was concerned about safety the most. But when I got out of my vehicle, my concerns quickly shifted onto the torturous heat. It was 107 degrees with scorching heat that was piercing into my skin. I couldn't believe that this was the weather we were going to work in. Our team headed onto the field to get work started. As we began working, all I could think about was water and cooler temperatures. The longer I worked the more I began to feel strength leaving my body. At around noon that day, I couldn't take it anymore. I just wanted to hide indoors and recharge because my strength was gone. I felt helpless.

Sin makes us helpless. Holding onto sin can often make us feel like we being scorched by sizzling summer heat. This can make us uncomfortable—and at times, powerless. The power of sin is heavy as it drains us from the inside out. When kept inside, sin begins to slowly eat away at our soul, crushing us until we cannot function anymore. In this state we become vulnerable and susceptible to further behaviors of sin. James, the half-brother of Jesus, writes, "Then, after desire has conceived, it gives birth to sin; and sin, when it is full-grown, gives birth to death" (Jas 1:15). The goal of sin is to bring death to people. This is the painful reality of the world that we live in. Sin is everywhere. Sin needs to be revealed so that it can be healed. The longer it is kept in, the more we waste away. This is what David emphasizes in Psalm 32.

David writes, "When I kept silent, my bones wasted away through my groaning all day long. For day and night your hand was heavy on me; my strength was sapped as in the heat of summer" (Ps 32:3–4). The reality is that sin is heavy. It pains us. It hurts us and it hurts those around us. When sin is withheld from God and others, it begins to feel as though our bones are wasting away. We feel a heavy burden that presses upon us, eliminating the very strength within us. Sin will find its way out of us one way or another. Holding it in can be the worst possible thing for us. Sin weighs us down. It makes us feel like there are bricks on our shoulders. We feel burdened and alone. The reason these experiences take place is because sin isn't something that is meant to be kept inside of us. Sin is meant to be confessed and surrendered so that we may experience freedom in Christ. Jesus died for a purpose and that purpose was to forgive our sin, uniting us into an eternal relationship with him.

Sin that is not surrendered destroys us from within. We must be a people who recognize our wrongdoing, trusting in God's faithfulness to forgive. The enemy is busy at work trying to fill us with discouragement and evil thoughts. We need to confront the enemy by allowing Christ to be our victory over sin and death. We cannot conquer sin on our own. Surrendering our sin upon Christ sets us free from pain, guilt, and shame. This is what David implies in Psalm 32; when sin is hidden, it is destroys us and consumes us. There is power in confessing sin. David kept his sin from God, experiencing the personal suffering of unrepentant sin. Once David confessed his sin, he experienced true forgiveness through God's incredible grace.

Grace > the Enemy

The enemy is very real and at work. He is constantly looking to deteriorate that which is good. His hope is to ruin the lives of people. His hope is to separate people from the love of God. His hope is to have victory over us—leading us into temptation and causing us to sin. The enemy wants to destroy our lives and lead us into darkness—a place without hope. So often, people fall into the darkness that the enemy leads them into. Once this darkness overtakes us, sin begins to consume us. Peter wrote about the characteristics and role of the enemy in the Book of 1 Peter, which helps us understand what we need to watch out for:

> Be alert and of sober mind. Your enemy the devil prowls around like a roaring lion looking for someone to devour. (1 Pet 5:10, NIV)

The enemy is on a mission to bring separation between humanity and God. Often, this works. This is why we must be alert and sober-minded. The moment we aren't alert and aware of the enemy is the moment he can devour us. A great way to counter the enemy is by consistently looking for ways to confess our sin and lean into God's grace. While there is still time, let us turn from our wickedness and trust that the Lord will set us free from our transgressions. When we're hurt, broken, and feel like we've dug ourselves into sin, there is profound truth that may be found in our heavenly Father's heart towards his creatures. Specifically, God empathizes with his creation. He enters into our very space and offers us his grace, love, and, ultimately, reconciliation to himself. This beautiful picture of grace is demonstrated throughout the entire narrative of Scripture.

Adam and Eve

Sin was birthed into the world through Adam and Eve. God gave them everything to enjoy with one particular restriction—eating the fruit from the tree of the knowledge of good and evil. As we may know, Adam and Eve disobeyed God. Even in their disobedience, God had a plan for redeeming their wrongs. He did this by foreshadowing his coming into the world by way of the Son, Jesus Christ (Gen 3:15). Let's think about this for a moment . . . God creates the world; creates mankind; and gives mankind all things to enjoy. He made an ask that mankind simply does not partake in eating the fruit from the tree of the knowledge of good and evil. Mankind fell for the temptation of the enemy and participated in rebellion towards God. God's solution? Grace. He had a plan. And his plan was to offer a second chance to all who would disobey him. This plan was the gospel. God demonstrates his grace through the gospel of Jesus Christ. There is nothing that we can do to deserve this, nothing that we do to earn it, yet God, in his grace and love towards his people, offers this as a beautiful and free gift to all who would choose to believe. God freely gives this gift of sacrificial love, mercy, and forgiveness. When Adam and Eve decided to disobey and sin against God, God offered his grace.

Noah

After sin was introduced into the world by way of Adam and Eve, though God had a solution in mind, he was angered. He was angered at all of the wickedness that existed and was transpiring due to humankind:

> The Lord saw how great the wickedness of the human race had become on the earth, and that every inclination of the thoughts of the human heart was only evil all the time. The Lord regretted that he had made human beings on the earth, and his heart was deeply troubled. So the Lord said, "I will wipe from the face of the earth the human race I have created—and with them the animals, the birds and the creatures that move along the ground—for

I regret that I have made them." But Noah found favor in the eyes of the Lord.

This is the account of Noah and his family. Noah was a righteous man, blameless among the people of his time, and he walked faithfully with God. Noah had three sons: Shem, Ham and Japheth.

Now the earth was corrupt in God's sight and was full of violence. God saw how corrupt the earth had become, for all the people on earth had corrupted their ways. So God said to Noah, "I am going to put an end to all people, for the earth is filled with violence because of them. I am surely going to destroy both them and the earth. So make yourself an ark of cypress wood; make rooms in it and coat it with pitch inside and out. (Gen 6:5–14, NIV)

Clearly there is anger in the Lord's heart. He was angered because the very humanity that he had created displayed evil within. This evil was a result of the sin that existed. But there was hope in a man named Noah. Noah was a righteous man as the text tells us (Gen 6:9). He was faithful and walked with God. God knew that he could count on Noah in the midst of all the tragedy that was taking place with the rest of humanity. Noah was God's plan of demonstrating grace to all. He called Noah to build an ark and gather all sorts of animals, as well as Noah's family (Gen 7:1). Later, the earth was flooded and Noah persevered through the flood because God remembered him (Gen 7:24—8:1). God removed the flood waters and made a covenant with Noah:

"Whenever I bring clouds over the earth and the rainbow appears in the clouds, I will remember my covenant between me and you and all living creatures of every kind. Never again will the waters become a flood to destroy all life. Whenever the rainbow appears in the clouds, I will see it and remember the everlasting covenant between God and all living creatures of every kind on the earth." (Gen 9:14–16, NIV)

This covenant was a demonstration of the grace of God. God was faithful to his promise and has never flooded the earth again. Though sin existed in the world through the wickedness of humanity, God—in his grace—offered another opportunity for mankind. When humanity decided to choose evil and wickedness, God offered his grace.

David

This man who seemed to be perfectly fit to be a follower of God and representative of true Christian character was far from it. David lived a lifestyle that wouldn't necessarily be considered "God-honoring." He lusted, killed, lied, and consistently fell short of God's standards. In light of other biblical characters, David was not doing too well. Although David was not doing well according to God's standards of Christian character, God continued to pursue him. In response, David became a man after God's own heart. He saw that God loved him no matter his shortcomings. Certainly there were consequences in the life of David, but God showered him with his love and mercy. David went down as one of the most prolific Christians in church history. Though David fell short of the glory of God, God offered his unmerited favor upon David and his life. David lived a life of missing the mark—and as he came to his senses, he proactively surrendered his sin to God. One of the most famous psalms records the sin that is surrendered by David unto God:

> Have mercy on me, O God,
>   according to your unfailing love;
> according to your great compassion
>   blot out my transgressions.
> Wash away all my iniquity
>   and cleanse me from my sin.
>
> For I know my transgressions,
>   and my sin is always before me.
> Against you, you only, have I sinned
>   and done what is evil in your sight;

so you are right in your verdict
   and justified when you judge.
Surely I was sinful at birth,
   sinful from the time my mother conceived me.
Yet you desired faithfulness even in the womb;
   you taught me wisdom in that secret place.

Cleanse me with hyssop, and I will be clean;
   wash me, and I will be whiter than snow.
Let me hear joy and gladness;
   let the bones you have crushed rejoice.
Hide your face from my sins
   and blot out all my iniquity.

Create in me a pure heart, O God,
   and renew a steadfast spirit within me.
Do not cast me from your presence
   or take your Holy Spirit from me.
Restore to me the joy of your salvation
   and grant me a willing spirit, to sustain me.
   (Ps 51:1–12, NIV)

This psalm indicates David's repentant heart as he seeks God for forgiveness. Imagine if our approach to sin was like David's. Yes, he made mistakes. Many of them. Yet David knew that apart from the grace of God, there would be no forgiveness. He chose to surrender his sin as God would faithfully forgive and renew his spirit.

We do not deserve God's grace. We are broken and hurting from self-inflicted wounds. Sin is a natural tendency of all humanity. We cling to it because it is appealing. Sin is evil masked as good. If left unconfessed, sin begins to devour and destroy us from within. It can shatter us and make us numb to what God intended for us. The psalm of David helps us see that sin must be revealed and, ultimately, it will be forgiven. We need to do our part in surrendering our sin to God. God in his faithful love towards us forgives our sin through the sacrificial body and blood of Christ Jesus. Christ surrendered his life on the cross for us so that we would surrender our sin upon him. He takes our sin upon himself—freely—to unite us in a beautiful relationship with God the Father Almighty. What once was broken because of the curse of sin is now mended by the grace of the cross.

Questions for Reflection

1. How do you respond to the weight of your sin?

2. What makes you think that your sin is too big for God to handle?

3. Read Psalm 51 as a prayer towards God and a posture of surrendering your sin.

4. How did your experience praying Psalm 51 draw you to humility?

5. What practical measures can you take moving forward with surrendering sin?

Reflections on Chapter 3 | **Sin Surrendered**

"Christ surrendered his life on the cross for us so that we would surrender our sin upon him."

Part Two

Healing

Chapter 4 | **True Repentance**

*Then I acknowledged my sin to you and did not cover up
my iniquity. I said, "I will confess my transgressions to
the Lord." And you forgave the guilt of my sin.*

—PSALM 32:5

R oad trips can be very fun. You can get together with some of
your best friends, your spouse, or your family, and head out on
an adventure. Before you head out though, you must prepare for the
journey. This usually involves consulting a map or GPS prior to one's
departure. We do this in hopes of taking a strategic way to either get
there faster, or to experience the more scenic route.

When my wife and I were dating in college, we would try and
visit each other frequently. I was studying in downtown Chicago,
while she was studying in rural Indiana. The commute that stood
between us was approximately three to four hours. One weekend,
I prepared my belongings and hit the road as I began my journey
to visit her. During my travels, I crossed the Illinois/Indiana border
and began following the signs towards 65 South, which would lead
me on a venture towards Indianapolis. I began to get very comfort-
able on my trip and was lost in deep, profound thought (per usual).
All of a sudden I came to a realization that I was traveling in the
complete opposite direction of Indianapolis—headed northbound. I
quickly looked for the nearest exit so that I could turn around—getting back on track to where I was supposed to be going.

Sin is what pulls us into the wrong direction in life. It makes
empty promises and gives us false hope. When we chase after it,
we run further and further from the will of God. Turning from

our sin and never looking back on it is something that we must strive for each day. And this is exactly what God calls us to: repentance. Charles Haddon Spurgeon, an English Baptist preacher, once said in a sermon:

> Repentance is a discovery of the evil of sin, a mourning that we have committed it, a resolution to forsake it. It is, in fact, a change of mind of a very deep and practical character, which makes the man love what once he hated, and hate what once he loved.[1]

> Repentance is to leave the sins we loved before, and show that we in earnest grieve, by doing so no more.[2]

Repentance is completely turning from our sin and looking to Jesus in faith. We will come back to repentance at the end of this chapter, but in order for us to understand and embrace the importance of repentance, we must first learn about the *power* and *need* of confession.

David's Confession

After David became the king of Israel, he became a victor of many battles. Scripture records:

> David defeated the Philistines and subdued them, and he took Metheg Ammah from the control of the Philistines.
> David also defeated the Moabites. He made them lie down on the ground and measured them off with a length of cord. Every two lengths of them were put to death, and the third length was allowed to live. So the Moabites became subject to David and brought him tribute.
> Moreover, David defeated Hadadezer son of Rehob, king of Zobah, when he went to restore his monument at the Euphrates River. David captured a thousand of his chariots, seven thousand charioteers and twenty

1. Spurgeon, *Complete Works*, 247.
2. Spurgeon, *Complete Works*, 247.

thousand foot soldiers. He hamstrung all but a hundred of the chariot horses.

When the Arameans of Damascus came to help Hadadezer king of Zobah, David struck down twenty-two thousand of them. He put garrisons in the Aramean kingdom of Damascus, and the Arameans became subject to him and brought tribute. The Lord gave David victory wherever he went.

David took the gold shields that belonged to the officers of Hadadezer and brought them to Jerusalem. From Tebah and Berothai, towns that belonged to Hadadezer, King David took a great quantity of bronze.

When Tou king of Hamath heard that David had defeated the entire army of Hadadezer, he sent his son Joram to King David to greet him and congratulate him on his victory in battle over Hadadezer, who had been at war with Tou. Joram brought with him articles of silver, of gold and of bronze.

King David dedicated these articles to the Lord, as he had done with the silver and gold from all the nations he had subdued: Edom and Moab, the Ammonites and the Philistines, and Amalek. He also dedicated the plunder taken from Hadadezer son of Rehob, king of Zobah.

And David became famous after he returned from striking down eighteen thousand Edomites in the Valley of Salt.

He put garrisons throughout Edom, and all the Edomites became subject to David. The Lord gave David victory wherever he went. (2 Sam 8:1–14, NIV)

It appeared that there was no battle that David would not win. He was strong. He had the right people around him. And the Lord gave David victory wherever he went (2 Sam 8:14). As David was perceived as someone who could not lose any kind of battle, he was confronted with one of the most challenging battles of his life: *the battle of temptation.*

During the springtime, when kings would go to war, David found himself in a bad situation. He found a woman bathing on the roof. This woman was Bathsheba. David had sent someone to find out more information about her. Once his messenger came back, David was informed that this woman was "the daughter of Eliam and the wife of Uriah the Hittite" (2 Sam 11:3). David quickly proceeded to sleep with Bathsheba. From an outsider's perspective, David was a strong warrior, a great leader, a loyal friend, and a faithful follower after God's own heart. Yet David's concerns seemed to be more focused on selfishness, lust, and ultimately falling into temptation. He was internally broken, yet he wasn't aware of it quite yet.

God in his grace sought to bring David a wake up call. He used the prophet Nathan to speak truth into David's life:

> The Lord sent Nathan to David. When he came to him, he said, "There were two men in a certain town, one rich and the other poor. The rich man had a very large number of sheep and cattle, but the poor man had nothing except one little ewe lamb he had bought. He raised it, and it grew up with him and his children. It shared his food, drank from his cup and even slept in his arms. It was like a daughter to him.
>
> "Now a traveler came to the rich man, but the rich man refrained from taking one of his own sheep or cattle to prepare a meal for the traveler who had come to him. Instead, he took the ewe lamb that belonged to the poor man and prepared it for the one who had come to him."
>
> David burned with anger against the man and said to Nathan, "As surely as the Lord lives, the man who did this must die! He must pay for that lamb four times over, because he did such a thing and had no pity."
>
> Then Nathan said to David, "You are the man! This is what the Lord, the God of Israel, says: 'I anointed you king over Israel, and I delivered you from the hand of Saul. I gave your master's house to you, and your master's wives into your arms. I gave you all Israel and Judah. And if all this had been too little, I would have given you even more. Why did you despise the word of the Lord by doing what is evil in his eyes? You struck down Uriah the Hittite with the sword and took his wife to be your own. You killed him with the sword of the Ammonites. Now, therefore, the sword will never depart from your house,

because you despised me and took the wife of Uriah the Hittite to be your own.'

"This is what the Lord says: 'Out of your own household I am going to bring calamity on you. Before your very eyes I will take your wives and give them to one who is close to you, and he will sleep with your wives in broad daylight. You did it in secret, but I will do this thing in broad daylight before all Israel.'"

Then David said to Nathan, "I have sinned against the Lord."

Nathan replied, "The Lord has taken away your sin. You are not going to die." (2 Sam 12:1–13, NIV)

David came to a realization that what he did was terribly wrong. He committed a sin against God, Bathsheba, and Uriah the Hittite. David had fallen in the battle of temptation, yet God used Nathan to draw the sin out in David's life. This ultimately led David to do his part in owning his wrongdoing—offering up his confession to the Lord.

Our Confession

Confession bears the power to set us free. Although there may be fear in confession, it exposes our weakness and demonstrates a desire and a need to change. We cannot cling to the fear of confessing our sin as this can force us to hide the very thing that God wants to heal within us. The healing process can only begin if we are vulnerable enough to admit our wrongdoing. God yearns for our sin to be confessed and dealt with—so that we may experience freedom in the gospel of Christ. Yet, so often we experience the temptation of hiding in our sin because we have a fear that our guilt and shame will no longer be sheltered. If we feed into this temptation, we begin to experience a weighty burden upon our shoulders. God does not intend for this. Rather, God desires to liberate us from the unconfessed baggage and sin patterns in our life. In order to fully experience God's intent for putting our sin to death, we must recognize our need for repentance. Ultimately, our sin is covered by the work of Christ Jesus on the cross.

But in order for us to fully embrace this reality, we need to do our part in uncovering our sin. We cannot continue covering our sin as God has already uncovered it. Thus confession must be at the forefront of our lifestyle as we adopt a posture of offering ourselves up to God. David exhibited this posture before God when he acknowledged his iniquity.

David was working through repentance in his own life when he wrote Psalm 32. Feeling the weight of guilt and shame—knowing he needed to confess—David experienced the suffering of his unconfessed sin and the burden that it brought upon his life. He coveted forgiveness that only God could offer and that would ultimately free him from the guilt in his life. He knew that he could not continue living in this way. He wanted to experience the freedom that comes in God's grace. God's desire is for all people to experience his forgiveness by way of his grace and mercy. And David knew this because he had a great relationship with God. In David's moment of weakness, he decided that he was going to lean on the strength of God's grace. David repented. God forgave. David was released from his guilt and shame. Even though David felt unworthy to receive God's forgiveness, God received his true repentance and used David regardless of what he had done. True repentance brings authentic forgiveness. David chose to repent of his sin, leading him to confess.

Grace

Grace is freely given, not earned. God has a passion for broken people. He was willing to crucify his one and only Son so that, through our repentance, we would join the work of God in redeeming humanity back to himself. This is the work of the gospel. The gospel intends to heal even the worst of sinners, so that Christ Jesus can offer forgiveness and reconciliation to all. The apostle Paul writes:

> I thank Christ Jesus our Lord, who has given me strength, that he considered me trustworthy, appointing me to his service. Even though I was once a blasphemer

and a persecutor and a violent man, I was shown mercy because I acted in ignorance and unbelief. The grace of our Lord was poured out on me abundantly, along with the faith and love that are in Christ Jesus.

Here is a trustworthy saying that deserves full acceptance: Christ Jesus came into the world to save sinners—of whom I am the worst. But for that very reason I was shown mercy so that in me, the worst of sinners, Christ Jesus might display his immense patience as an example for those who would believe in him and receive eternal life. (1 Tim 1:12–16)

One could only imagine how unworthy of Christ's grace and forgiveness Paul felt. He tells Timothy that he was a blasphemer, a persecutor, and a violent man. What Paul says next is true of us all, "The grace of our Lord was poured out on me abundantly, along with the faith and love that are in Christ Jesus" (1 Tim 1:14). God didn't have this miraculous plan of Paul getting his life in order, and only then God would offer his great grace on Paul. His grace was given to Paul regardless. When Paul noticed and received this grace from God, he couldn't help but repent for his wrongdoing.

Our lives are similar to Paul's. We have all wronged God due to our sin against him. We continue to wrong God—whether Christian or not—as sin continues to flow out of us. The truth is that we cannot escape sin in a sinful world. It is always going to be present. God's plan is that in Christ we may experience the forgiveness of sin, setting us free from the sin that is keeping us in bondage. This does not mean that in Christ we become perfect human beings that never sin again. We continue to sin because we are broken. Yet the blood of Christ washes our sin away each day. Our past does not define who we are or who we will become. As believers in the Lord Jesus Christ, we receive forgiveness through his atoning work on the cross. The work is finished. It can no longer be altered. God is constantly lavishing his grace on us regardless of our behavior or circumstance. Our response must be repentance. When we truly recognize the grace and forgiveness that is offered to us in Christ, we ought to confess our sin and trust that the blood of Christ has forgiven us.

Paul was a man unworthy of God's love. He had a terrible reputation. He was an active sinner. He was among the least qualified to be a servant of the Lord Jesus. After encountering Jesus, Paul knew that there was no way he could remain the person he once was. He encountered the grace of Christ and repented of his sin. Paul was never the same again. He was transformed into a child of God. Though he was unworthy, God extended his love to Paul by giving his Son, Jesus Christ, so that Paul would be forgiven.

When we feel unworthy of God's love we must cling to the forgiveness of Christ. The truth is that all are unworthy of God's love. Yet the grace of the Lord Jesus is freely given to us, which allows us to indeed be worthy in the sight of God. This is not by our own doing. We cannot earn God's love by doing good things for God. He has done all of the work on our behalf. He sent his one and only Son into the world to redeem it of sin. God in Christ has done the greatest work in human history and invites us to participate in an everlasting relationship with him. The work of the cross has engrafted believers in Christ to experience freedom from sin. We are no longer bound to our guilt and shame. We are set free in Christ, which allows us to participate in the kingdom of God forever.

Repentance

In order for us to participate in the work of Christ, we must first recognize our need for repentance. In Christ, we have already been forgiven. Our job then is to receive this forgiveness, being fully assured that the blood of Jesus has washed us clean. This truth sets us free from the bondage that we may be in. In the Gospel of John, Jesus told a group of believing Jews that holding to his teachings will help them know the truth about who he is. Knowing the truth about who Jesus is would ultimately set them free—free from their sin. Jesus says that everyone is a slave to sin and in need of healing and restoration (John 8:34). This healing and restoration is found in the person and work of Jesus Christ. If the Son of God, Jesus Christ, sets us free, then we will be free indeed (John 8:36).

This freedom is experienced through the repentance of our sin. Matthew's Gospel records Jesus saying, "Repent, for the kingdom of heaven has come near" (Matt 4:17). Jesus is saying that one's life must portray a complete change of attitude and thought concerning sin and righteousness. This shows strength and maturity in our pursuit of true repentance. Allowing ourselves to embrace the gospel of Jesus Christ develops in us a change of heart. Our sin becomes the very thing that we begin to hate. This is the overflow of the gospel within us, which is a sign of spiritual maturity and growth. When we repent of our sin, we allow the work of Christ to mold us into the image of God. This image is represented by our desire and willingness to practice the spiritual discipline of repentance—turning away from our sin. As we turn from our sin, we're able to become more like Christ Jesus. The difficulty is that we can never accomplish the repentance of our sin on our own. We need the help of the one who conquered all sin.

Imperfect humanity is in need of a perfect redeemer. This is the only way restoration is brought between a broken people and a Holy God. Since humanity is broken—unable to display perfection—God himself became incarnate, by way of Christ Jesus, so that he could live a perfect life on our behalf. This is an essential act of God because it determines the future of the human race. Apart from Christ, we are guilty of our sin, deserving the penalty of death. In Christ, we are redeemed from our sin, as we are united into a perfect and holy relationship with God the Father Almighty. This is accomplished solely based on the person and work of Christ Jesus. As we put our faith and trust in Christ, we are forgiven. Healing from our sin begins with Jesus. After this healing process begins, it will remain throughout our lifetime as we embrace a posture of becoming more like Christ, which is sanctification. Trusting in Christ molds us into the image of Christ through our obedience. When we fall short of becoming more like Christ, we are forgiven, restored, and the grace of God pours out upon us—constantly making us new. The matter of life-change does not solely rest on us but on Christ as the founder and perfecter of our faith (Heb 12:2, ESV). True repentance allows the power of the gospel to make us new and whole again. Let us lean into Christ. Rely on him. Trust in him. He will change you. He will heal you.

Questions for Reflection

1. What makes it difficult to receive forgiveness when you know you don't deserve it?

2. How do you think repentance can bring about healing in your life?

3. Take a moment to repent from a particular sin that's been on your heart.

4. Do you have faith that God has forgiven you and given you a clean slate? Why or why not?

5. How can you move forward with confidence, knowing that God intends to lavish his love upon you?

Reflections on Chapter 4 | **True Repentance**

"True repentance allows the power of the gospel to make us new and whole again."

Chapter 5 | The Faithfulness of God

*Therefore let all the faithful pray to you while
you may be found; surely the rising of the mighty
waters will not reach them.*

—PSALM 32:6

I used to be decent at basketball. Now that I am of older age, it is much more difficult for me to play without experiencing aches and pains throughout my body the next morning. The funny thing is, I'm not that old—yet. But it's simply not the way it used to be. As someone who grew up playing basketball, I would naturally have the desire to try out for teams, wanting to play the sport I love. I remember my high school tryouts. I walked in as a fragile, thin, awkwardly tall-looking human being who wanted nothing less than to make the freshman basketball team. Fast forward a few weeks: I did indeed make the freshman basketball team. I was thrilled. Excited. I was ready to work hard and make a difference on the court for my team. A few weeks into playing freshman basketball, my team was participating in our daily practices. We would have shooting drills, conditioning, scrimmages, and testing out various plays that we could run. As we were working on our plays, I began to move into the space where I needed to be for that particular play. As I was running I began to lose my breath. Everything that I saw began to appear in slow motion. I could hear my heartbeat as if it were beating through my ears. I started to collapse on the court. All of a sudden, I found myself laying on the basketball court with a heart rate that was through the roof. My coaches contacted the trainers and the trainers contacted 911.

Whatever was happening to me required *urgent* medical attention at the time. I was diagnosed with Supraventricular tachycardia. Though treatable, the situation required immediate action.

Psalm 32:6

David just finished writing on repentance before he uttered an *urgent* plea. After David's repentance to the Lord, he received forgiveness for his iniquity. He knew that God was faithful to forgive, and his sin was released. After experiencing this, David desired that all would follow suit and offer up their transgressions to the Lord. He made the request, emphasizing urgency:

"Therefore let all the faithful pray to you while you may be found; surely the rising of the mighty waters will not reach them" (Ps 32:6). This text begins with the word *therefore*, meaning that it is directly linked to the previous passage. Sin divides us from God, and as we become humble enough to acknowledge our brokenness that we're living in before a Holy God, we are able to demonstrate only a glimpse of what it looks like to be faithful. Acknowledging our sin demonstrates an act of obedience and humility. And when it comes to our spiritual journey, we must seek and turn to God with *urgency*. Through God's mercy, we're able to approach the throne of Grace, which reveals our wickedness. Therefore in our confession of sin, we are able to pray to God, who is able to hear and forgive us. The *urgency* of this text suggests that we turn to God in prayer while he may still be found. While the opportunity remains, let us seek and desire God's presence, and in doing so, let us remember that he alone can heal our pain and brokenness. There can be a tendency for us to turn to the substances of deception as a way to "cure" our pain and brokenness. We look to drugs, alcohol, pharmaceuticals, acceptance, idolatry, people-pleasing—just to name a few—as methods of fabricating the deep pain within us. These things do more harm than good, and, more often than not, they overpromise and underdeliver. It can be easy to fall into the trap of worldly pleasures and lose sight of God's holiness.

Sin and Holiness

It is crucial that we understand the mortality of our human nature. Here on earth it may appear that our lives will go on forever, yet this is just not the case. Everyone is destined to die on earth, and death is a direct result of sin. Paul writes in his letter to the Romans, "For the wages of sin is death, but the gift of God is eternal life in Christ Jesus our Lord" (Rom 6:23). The world may appear to be deceptive, which can ultimately lead us into the path of eternal separation from God. When we are unfaithful, God is faithful. God is set apart from humanity's sin nature. This means that the God of the universe is a holy God. And because God is holy, his desire is that we, too, may live a life of holiness. When sin is knocking on our door we must desire to resist. This is what sets us apart from those who live wickedly. The author of Hebrews addresses the idea of holiness, with the desire that all who are being made holy would be able to see the work of the Lord in and through their lives. The author writes, "Make every effort to live in peace with everyone and to be holy; without holiness no one will see the Lord" (Heb 12:14). When our desire is to set ourselves apart from sin, people notice. Something changes within our very being as we long to be more like Christ Jesus. A desire to pursue holiness is the desire to be more like Christ. Chip Ingram, in his book *The Real God*, describes holiness beautifully:

> The dictionary offers definitions like "to divide," "to mark off," and "to set apart from all else" to describe the uses of the word *holy*. It's the opposite of profane, common, or ordinary. To be holy is to be different, distinct, or unique. The English roots refer to that which is whole, healthy, happy, sound, complete, and unspoiled. The word holy eventually came to mean "spiritually pure, sacred, untainted by evil, sinless."[1]

He goes on to say:

> When applied to God, holiness is that which divides him from everyone and everything else. It is the quality of

1. Ingram, *The Real God*, 121.

"awesome mystery" in God's being, his essential nature and character that make him different, distinct, and unique from any other thing or person in the universe.[2]

God is faithful in being holy. He is set apart from us. This is why God can be faithful to us even when we're unfaithful to him. He desires that we may be people who are in constant communication with him so that we can become more like his Son, Jesus Christ. At face value, we are not holy. We cannot achieve holiness. It is only by being in Christ that we can become set apart for the kingdom of God. Desiring to become more like the Son of God gives us a more beautiful picture of what it looks like to be faithful in this journey called *life*. We need to pursue faithfulness in our commitment to Christ so that holiness becomes a part of who we are. Christ's very holiness resides in us by way of the Holy Spirit. The Spirit of God conforms us to the image of Christ so that we may lead others into the knowledge of Christ. While there is still time, let us turn to our loving God and rest in his unchanging grace. His grace will give us strength. His grace will give us a new perspective. His grace will lead us into a journey of faithfulness. And his grace will give us *urgency* to plead with God for the reconciliation of our sin and the reconciliation of the brokenness that exists in our community, city, state, country, and world.

Faithfulness

God's faithfulness is also expressed through the way that he meets us exactly where we're at. He desires that we too may be faithful in recognizing that he alone can heal our transgressions. This realization helps us become more like the image-bearers of Christ that we were made to be. Christ in his very nature is faithful. Therefore if we desire to embody the faithfulness of Christ, we must surrender ourselves to him who is able to lead us in the way of faithfulness. We will see that in doing this, God—in his grace—will continue to work in our hearts, conforming us to his precious image. God

2. Ingram, *The Real God*, 121–22.

is faithful in offering forgiveness to us. Because of this, we must seek to be fellow forgivers in the gospel. Knowing what Christ has done for us ought to help us and guide us into a lifestyle of offering forgiveness towards others.

David and Us

David's desire was to encourage his readers to understand the depth and weight of their sin. In doing so, one may realize the power of God's faithfulness in forgiving sin. This can only be experienced while the opportunity still remains. No one knows the day or the hour that Christ shall return to take his people with him. No one knows the day or the hour of his or her own time concluding on this earth, thus there is urgency in being faithful in our prayers to God. There is urgency in the restoration of our relationships with others. We must offer our petitions to our holy God, who is longing to hear from us. God desires our honest and earnest prayers. He is faithful to receive, answer, and forgive us of our sin—if only we would realize the significance of our much-needed repentance.

David sums up what he has written in the previous five verses here in Psalm 32:6. "Therefore let all the faithful pray to you while you may be found; surely the rising of the mighty waters will not reach them." Due to the faithfulness of God in his forgiveness towards us, let all the faithful pray to Yahweh while Yahweh may be found. The opportunity still remains to rejoice in God's faithfulness by surrendering ourselves to his glory and his plan for us. Time still remains for us to flee from our sin and run towards our Savior God, who longs to restore us to himself. This is accomplished because God is faithful. When we pray to him, the Holy Spirit enables us to receive the forgiveness that is offered to us through the work of Christ Jesus on the cross. In the forgiveness found in the grace of God, we are made clean; we are made new; we are made his. Time and time again, God is seeking to meet the needs of his people, even though they betray and turn their backs on him. Yet his empathy is wider than any form of our disobedience towards him. He extends his grace and loves people no matter what! Let us respond to this grace with vulnerability and honesty, being receptive to this free gift from God. Let us be faithful in our posture towards God by being bold, humble, and honest before him. While there is still time, let us receive grace and offer grace. This is a critical element of the Christian faith.

As we read Scripture, we see God use the most broken of people to accomplish his purpose in this world. When humanity chooses to be unfaithful and rebellious towards God, God still chooses to faithfully use a broken humanity for his purpose and glory. We aren't forgiven because of anything that we do. We're forgiven because of everything Christ has done. This is the faithfulness of God that is never-ending. Let us lean into this truth as we continue to experience the profound mystery of the gospel.

Questions for Reflection

1. How have you seen the faithfulness of God in your life?

2. How is God faithful in the midst of our sin?

3. In what areas of your life can you lean into God's faithfulness?

4. How can you pursue being set apart for Christ?

5. What have you learned from God's faithfulness and holiness?

Reflections on Chapter 5 | **The Faithfulness of God**

"We aren't forgiven because of anything that we do. We're forgiven because of everything Christ has done."

Chapter 6 | The Lord Is Our Refuge

*You are my hiding place; you will protect me from
trouble and surround me with songs of deliverance.*

—PSALM 32:7

In 2011, native Chicagoans experienced something unusual.
Whether you prefer the term snowpocalypse or snowmageddon,
both are great for describing what transpired that year. Nearly two
feet of snow fell within a twenty-four-hour span, and approximately
one thousand vehicles were abandoned on Chicago's Lake Shore
Drive.[1] The city was a disaster, and many were trapped indoors.
Unless you were a thrill-seeker, you did everything in your power
to seek and remain in shelter. A shelter is a place of comfort and
protection as one seeks to be safe. We all have moments in our lives
when we seek to confine ourselves to our areas of safety, receiving
protection from various situations that may arise. Where do you
go for your place of comfort and peace? Where do you go for rest?
When you think of your place of refuge, what comes to mind?

It can be easy to find a refuge in the things of this world.
When unexpected circumstances impede our lives, we may have
a tendency to self-medicate with what this world has to offer. This
is the devastating nature of sin. It does not produce a solution for
circumstances in our lives; rather, it creates a deeper disfunction.
When situations arise and we are confronted with trials, God desires to be our refuge. He is our safe place. We must run to God
as our hiding place in times of trouble because he promises to be
everything that we need. God is all-satisfying. He is our living

1. Wambsgans, "Abandoned on LSD."

water, who nourishes us with what's necessary to get through the problems that we may face.

In verse 7 of Psalm 32, we see David demonstrate his faith in God's saving grace. Previously, David focused deeply on confession and repentance; now, David declares truth about who God is. He writes, "You are my hiding place; you will protect me from trouble and surround me with songs of deliverance" (Psalm 32:7, NIV). In the moments that David may have felt weak, weary, broken, and ashamed, God was his hiding place. He preserved David through his limitations. In David's limitations, God remained faithful to lavish David in his unending grace. To fail God time and time again, and still find refuge in him is why God's grace is complex. It is complex because it is unlike anything that anyone else can offer. He is a place of refuge despite how much we fail to measure up to his standards with our lives. He welcomes us with our aching sin and opens his arms for an embrace. We see this illustrated in one of the most distinguished parables in the New Testament.

The Parable of the Lost Son

Luke, a doctor in the New Testament, recorded key life events of Jesus and his teachings throughout his Gospel. Many of Jesus' teachings came by way of parable. A parable is a story that illustrates a lesson that Jesus was trying to teach. In chapter 15, Luke records three parables that Jesus gave when he was with the tax collectors, sinners, Pharisees, and teachers of the law, who were with him (Luke 15:1–2). The third parable helps us understand the refuge of the forgiving Father who is filled with grace. Luke writes:

> Jesus continued: "There was a man who had two sons. The younger one said to his father, 'Father, give me my share of the estate.' So he divided his property between them.
> "Not long after that, the younger son got together all he had, set off for a distant country and there squandered his wealth in wild living. After he had spent everything, there was a severe famine in that whole country, and he

began to be in need. So he went and hired himself out to a citizen of that country, who sent him to his fields to feed pigs. He longed to fill his stomach with the pods that the pigs were eating, but no one gave him anything.

"When he came to his senses, he said, 'How many of my father's hired servants have food to spare, and here I am starving to death! I will set out and go back to my father and say to him: Father, I have sinned against heaven and against you. I am no longer worthy to be called your son; make me like one of your hired servants.' So he got up and went to his father.

"But while he was still a long way off, his father saw him and was filled with compassion for him; he ran to his son, threw his arms around him and kissed him.

"The son said to him, 'Father, I have sinned against heaven and against you. I am no longer worthy to be called your son.'

"But the father said to his servants, 'Quick! Bring the best robe and put it on him. Put a ring on his finger and sandals on his feet. Bring the fattened calf and kill it. Let's have a feast and celebrate. *For this son of mine was dead and is alive again; he was lost and is found.*' So they began to celebrate.

"Meanwhile, the older son was in the field. When he came near the house, he heard music and dancing. So he called one of the servants and asked him what was going on. 'Your brother has come,' he replied, 'and your father has killed the fattened calf because he has him back safe and sound.'

"The older brother became angry and refused to go in. So his father went out and pleaded with him. But he answered his father, 'Look! All these years I've been slaving for you and never disobeyed your orders. Yet you never gave me even a young goat so I could celebrate with my friends. But when this son of yours who has squandered your property with prostitutes comes home, you kill the fattened calf for him!'

"'My son,' the father said, 'you are always with me, and everything I have is yours. But we had to celebrate and be glad, because this brother of yours was dead and is alive again; he was lost and is found.'" (Luke 15:11–32, NIV, emphasis added)

This parable gives us a glimpse of our God's gracious character. God is our hiding place, our place of shelter and comfort. The parable of the lost son displays divine forgiveness. The younger son wanted the father's inheritance, received it, and squandered everything. He lived a life that was filled with sin and selfishness. A lifetime of the father's accumulated inheritance—gone. The younger son was self-absorbed. He only wanted what was best for himself, neglecting the traditional patterns of inheritance (waiting for the father's death). Once he possessed these things, he thought his life was complete. He could indulge in any behavior he wanted. He partied. He was rebellious at the core. The people he loved seemed to not matter to him. He seemed to be well off, while enjoying himself and his desires. It took the younger son some time to realize that an inheritance was not all that mattered. When he came to his senses, he had the desire to repent of his sin and his way of life.

Meanwhile the older son followed all the rules and became jealous when the younger son came back home. Timothy Keller addresses this kind of character found in the religious people:

> Religious people commonly live very moral lives, but their goal is to get leverage over God, to control him, to put him in a position where they think he owes them. Therefore, despite all their ethical fastidiousness and piety, they are actually rebelling against his authority.[2]

The heart and character of both sons was inappropriate. One gained everything and then recklessly lost all that he had. The other was living in self-righteousness, thinking that he had it all together. Although both sons were at fault in their own way, the most profound component of this parable is arguably the role of the father.

Whether towards a strict rule-follower or a wayward child, the father demonstrated compassion and love. He was a place of

2. Keller, *The Prodigal God*, 44.

refuge regardless of the situation at hand. While the younger son was living in debauchery, the father waited for his return with hope, anticipation, and expectation. Luke records that "while he was still a long way off, his father saw him and was filled with compassion for him; he ran to his son, threw his arms around him and kissed him" (Luke 15:20, NIV). The father was a clear place of refuge in troubling times.

Our Refuge

Where do we run in times of trouble? Where do we go when all hope is lost? Regardless of our circumstances, do we find peace in the arms of our God the Father Almighty? God offers us himself as a source of healing. When troubling times arise, Christ is enough. When difficulty plagues our day-to-day lives, Christ is enough. God gives us himself as a source of comfort. We can participate in his everlasting love by submitting our lives to his plan and purpose for our life. This plan can and will include times of desperation and need, but God is good in the midst of those trying times. When we feel unworthy of God's forgiveness, he still offers it. God's grace and forgiveness is not conditioned upon on our behavior; rather, it is based on the person and work of Christ Jesus. There is nothing that we can do to earn God's favor. There is nothing that we can do to earn God's love. God, in his sovereign grace and mercy, reaches from the heavens and enters our very humanity to offer himself as our refuge and strength. Our response to this is to simply embrace the truth of who God is for us. Our response is to trust in God's plan of redemption through the blood of Jesus.

In the midst of a storm, we must seek shelter. Therefore, in troubling times, we must seek a refuge. And that refuge is Christ Jesus. He is our portion, our prize, and our salvation. In him, we have freedom. In him, we understand suffering at a greater degree. Apart from Christ, we are alone and broken. Christ offers us himself as our refuge. God's great gift to us is giving us the humanity of Jesus, so that he could bear our burdens with us. This gift offers us hope. This gift offers us peace. This gift offers us a life of gratitude and thanksgiving. Ultimately, this gift offers us a personal relationship that never fades. In Christ, we are given a relationship of eternal refuge. Will you lean into this truth and let the reality of the gospel give you hope—wherever you may be?

Questions for Reflection

1. Who or what do you consider to be your refuge in times of trouble?

2. What practical measures can you take in order to rely on God as your refuge and strength?

3. Where do you experience trouble in trusting the Lord as your refuge?

4. How can leaning into the Lord as your refuge allow you to experience God's peace and comfort?

Reflections on Chapter 6 | **The Lord Is Our Refuge**

"In Christ, we are given a relationship of eternal refuge."

Chapter 7 | God's Sovereign Guidance

I will instruct you and teach you in the way you should go; I will counsel you with my loving eye on you. Do not be like the horse or the mule, which have no understanding but must be controlled by bit and bridle or they will not come to you.

—PSALM 32:8–9

In 2015, I had the privilege of going to one of my favorite cities in the United States. I went to San Francisco. While I was in San Francisco, I noticed that there are many touristy things to do. One can visit Pier 39; bike the Golden Gate Bridge; visit the redwoods; and of course, walk through the world-famous prison—Alcatraz. Alcatraz was once a top-security federal prison that was home to many famous convicts. I was very fascinated by the history of this prison. My fascination led me to book a tour so that I could learn more about Alcatraz. After arriving on the island, I was uncertain of where I should go. People had the option of simply walking around and observing, or taking a guided tour through the prison. Since I had no clue where I was going, I thought the right choice would be to take a guided tour. During the tour of Alcatraz, the tour guide was very knowledgeable and helped me understand what each area of the prison was used for. I was also amazed at the amount these tour guides knew when it came to the facts about Alcatraz. Needless to say, I would have been wandering around, not knowing where I was going, or what I was doing, without the tour guide's help.

David has gone through many emotions while compiling this Psalm 32. He felt the weight of his sin and knew the the best action to take would be to confess to God. After doing this, he reflected on the goodness of God's forgiving grace. He then proceeded to acknowledge that God was his refuge. God was someone that David could approach, as he provides peace and comfort unlike anyone else. In Psalm 32:8–9, we see that God is our sovereign guidance. David relied on God to lead him and guide him throughout his life's journey. David is expressing his teachable spirit and God is honored by that. David knows that God is the ultimate source of guidance in this life—and so he leans in.

God is constantly watching us, desiring that we notice that he is the one who is in control. In his infinite wisdom, we're able to trust in him, even when things don't make sense. King Solomon demonstrates this posture in the famous proverb:

> Trust in the Lord with all your heart
>> and lean not on your own understanding;
> in all your ways submit to him,
>> and he will make your paths straight. (Prov 3:5–6, NIV)

Trusting God requires a posture of leaning not on our own understanding. We may not know the exact thing that God is leading us towards, but we must lean into him with our trust. This allows us to be teachable in moments of difficulty. When decisions arise, we know that God is truly in control and doing work in our lives. It's up to us to come to this realization so that we may allow God to work among us.

God Intervenes and Guides Paul

One of my favorite stories in the Bible is the transformation of Saul of Tarsus. Saul was one who murdered Christians. He was in no place to be considered a follower of God. The life he lived was a life of darkness and confusion—seeming like he had no purpose. But God, in his sovereignty, had a plan for Saul's life.

Luke recorded the beautiful story of God's sovereign guidance at work in the life of Saul:

> Meanwhile, Saul was still breathing out murderous threats against the Lord's disciples. He went to the high priest and asked him for letters to the synagogues in Damascus, so that if he found any there who belonged to the Way, whether men or women, he might take them as prisoners to Jerusalem. As he neared Damascus on his journey, suddenly a light from heaven flashed around him. He fell to the ground and heard a voice say to him, "Saul, Saul, why do you persecute me?"
>
> "Who are you, Lord?" Saul asked.
>
> "I am Jesus, whom you are persecuting," he replied. "Now get up and go into the city, and you will be told what you must do."
>
> The men traveling with Saul stood there speechless; they heard the sound but did not see anyone. Saul got up from the ground, but when he opened his eyes he could see nothing. So they led him by the hand into Damascus. For three days he was blind, and did not eat or drink anything.
>
> In Damascus there was a disciple named Ananias. The Lord called to him in a vision, "Ananias!"
>
> "Yes, Lord," he answered.
>
> The Lord told him, "Go to the house of Judas on Straight Street and ask for a man from Tarsus named Saul, for he is praying. In a vision he has seen a man named Ananias come and place his hands on him to restore his sight."
>
> "Lord," Ananias answered, "I have heard many reports about this man and all the harm he has done to your holy people in Jerusalem. And he has come here with authority from the chief priests to arrest all who call on your name."
>
> But the Lord said to Ananias, "Go! This man is my chosen instrument to proclaim my name to the Gentiles and their kings and to the people of Israel. I will show him how much he must suffer for my name."
>
> Then Ananias went to the house and entered it. Placing his hands on Saul, he said, "Brother Saul, the

Lord—Jesus, who appeared to you on the road as you were coming here—has sent me so that you may see again and be filled with the Holy Spirit." Immediately, something like scales fell from Saul's eyes, and he could see again. He got up and was baptized, and after taking some food, he regained his strength. (Acts 9:1–19, NIV)

Luke's record of Saul's conversion is incredible. How could someone's life be completely transformed? Only by the grace of God. After Saul's conversion, he would go on to pen the majority of what we today call the New Testament. God had a plan for Saul's life. That plan consisted of redeeming him from his sin and offering him a new identity in Christ. This new identity came with a name change. Saul became known as Paul. Paul would go on to live a radical life for the purpose of proclaiming the gospel to many. God would guide Paul's steps in revealing his will to him.

Paul's legacy is one that has been remembered for thousands of years. He continues to be one of the most influential Christians to ever live. We read his letters to see the work that Christ did in him and in the lives of others because of him. Paul found his strength in Christ Jesus—whom he represented throughout his life—post-conversion. God had a plan for Paul's life. When things seemed hopeless and irreversible, God intervened. God is faithful to step into people's lives and give them a hope. He has a sovereign plan to work in the midst of all people. Paul was someone that no one would think of as being a Christian. Yet God in his grace and mercy redeemed him, setting him apart for the ministry of the gospel.

God Intervenes and Guides Us

The God who worked in the lives of many biblical characters is the same God that is at work in us today. The God who redeemed Paul of his rebellious lifestyle is the same God that invites us into fellowship with him. God is sovereign over our lives. We need to come to a realization that he is truly in control and will provide us with his plan, if we submit our lives to him in obedience. He will guide our steps as we lean into him for strength and wisdom. God ultimately promises us himself, through his Son, Jesus Christ. Over two thousand years ago, God entered into human history and gave us a guide in his Son, Jesus Christ. God entered human flesh through Christ to show us the way. Christ was perfect and obedient to the will of the Father. The writer of Hebrews gives us a glimpse of this reality:

> During the days of Jesus' life on earth, he offered up prayers and petitions with fervent cries and tears to the one who could save him from death, and he was heard because of his reverent submission. Son though he was, he learned obedience from what he suffered and, once made perfect, he became the source of eternal salvation for all who obey him. (Hebrews 5:7–9, NIV)

Jesus Christ gave us the best example of what it looks like to follow God's guidance. The writer of Hebrews tells us that Jesus had a reverent submission to God the Father. Christ's submission to the Father is what it took to bring salvation to humanity. Christ's obedience required suffering as well. It wasn't an easy task to be the Son of God. Jesus dealt with many challenges that continued to draw him to the Father. His obedience was profound and made a lasting impact. F. F. Bruce, a Bible commentator, helps us further understand Christ's obedience through Christ's suffering:

> In what sense, then, did the Son of God learn obedience "by what he suffered"? We know the sense in which the words are true of us; we learn to be obedient because of the unpleasant consequences which follow disobedience. It was not so with him. As we are told later (10:7), he announced his dedication to the doing of God's will at his coming into the world. He set out from the start on the path of obedience to God, and learned by the sufferings which came his way in consequence just what obedience to God involved in practice in the conditions of human life on earth. Perhaps the obedient Servant of the Lord in Isa. 50:4–9 was in our author's mind. The Servant's eagerness to pay heed to the voice of God exposes him to ridicule and ill-treatment, but he accepts this as something

inseparable from his obedience: "The Lord Yahweh has opened my ear, and I was not rebellious, I turned not backward. I gave my back to the smiters, and my cheeks to those who pulled out the beard; I hid not my face from shame and spitting" (Isa. 50:5f.). So the sufferings which Jesus endured were the necessary price of his obedience— more than that, they were part and parcel of his obedience, the very means by which he fulfilled the will of God.[1]

Christ demonstrated the perfect example of what it looks like to follow the will of God through obedience. He fulfilled the will of God through his obedience as he took upon himself the cross at Calvary. He did this so that in him we would grasp faithful obedience to God. When we submit our lives to the will of God through our obedience, he will guide us in the direction he desires our lives to go. We can trust in God's plan and purpose because of what he did through Christ's obedience, on our behalf. As we discern God's will for us, we can trust that he has a perfect plan for our lives as he leads us to himself. Following Jesus means that we are able to participate in Christ's perfect submission to the Father by submitting our lives to Christ, who is our Lord. In our obedience, we're able to live a life that is led and guided by our sovereign God. Those who are led by the Spirit of God are the children of God (Rom 8:14, NIV). In our submission and obedience to God's plan for our life, we veto the right to control our destiny. There is freedom in this reality. When we make our own plans and aspirations we do our very best at maintaining them. If something doesn't work out according to our plan, we may be made angry; frustrated; bitter; confused; and perhaps questioning everything. It's in times like these that if we trusted in the Lord's plan for us, we would handle our failed plans differently. We would be aware that if the Lord himself is in control, then perhaps the thought or idea that we had wasn't the one that God had in mind for us. Rather, God is paving a perfect plan for us and we need to seek him for alignment. God guides the lives of many and wants to guide our lives. We need to do our part in choosing to trust in him with our lives. This will bring us peace as we trust in God's guidance.

---

1. Bruce, *Epistle to the Hebrews*, 131.

Sin and God's Guidance

This world is filled with a multitude of sin. We are all sinners who continue living in sin. Sin is something that God does not desire for us, yet he is sovereign over our sin. He knows what we are capable of when it comes to our disobedience. The question that we must ask is, does God will for us to sin? In his work *Christian Theology*, Millard J. Erickson wrote this, in regards to God's will:

> We must distinguish between two different senses of God's will, which we will refer to as God's "wish" (will 1) and God's "will" (will 2). The former is God's general intention, the values with which he is pleased. The latter is God's specific intention in a given situation, what he decided will actually occur. There are times, many of them, when God wills to permit, and thus to have occur, what he really does not wish. This is the case with sin. God does not desire sin to occur. There are occasions, however, when he simply says, in effect, "So be it," allowing a human to choose freely a sinful course of action. Joseph's treatment at the hands of his brothers did not please God; it was not consistent with what he is like. God did, however, will to permit it; he did not intervene to prevent it. And, interestingly enough, God used their action to produce the very thing it was intended to prevent—Joseph's ascendancy.[2]

Erickson helps us understand that God does not intend for us to sin. But God will use our sin—through the redemption of Jesus Christ—to bring about his sovereign plan. Even though we freely choose to disobey God in choosing sin, he is faithful to work in us, despite our sin nature. God's will and desire for our lives is to bring reconciliation to himself and others, through the work of Christ, so that we, too, might offer forgiveness towards those who have sinned against us. We see this in the Lord's Prayer as Jesus demonstrates to us a heart of forgiveness:

> "This, then, is how you should pray:
>
> "'Our Father in heaven,

2. Erickson, *Christian Theology*, 334.

hallowed be your name,

your kingdom come,

your will be done,

on earth as it is in heaven.

Give us today our daily bread.

And forgive us our debts,

as we also have forgiven our debtors.

And lead us not into temptation,

but deliver us from the evil one.'

For if you forgive other people when they sin against you, your heavenly Father will also forgive you. But if you do not forgive others their sins, your Father will not forgive your sins." (Matt 6:9–15, NIV)

Jesus says that if we forgive others' sin against us, our heavenly Father will also forgive us. At this point in the book, it is evident that individuals are born into this poison called *sin*. Naturally, we develop our own forms of sin. Yes, many can struggle and do struggle with the same sins as others. But each individual has their own key struggle(s) with a particular sin. Our desire must be to kill that sin in our life. In order for us to begin this process, we need Christ with us. Christ alone can and will take away our sin upon himself. If we are willing to admit that we are, indeed, in need of him as our Lord, he can help us work through our sin. He can help us conquer our sin. He can help us receive forgiveness for our sin through him. And if we truly lean into this goodness called grace, we can be taught—by Christ—how to forgive others. See, God has this plan of redemption that he wants us to participate in. Receiving forgiveness can be difficult for some, but it's there, nonetheless. Whether or not we feel worthy of God's grace, he will still lavish it upon us. This is the beauty of the gospel and, ultimately, the beauty of Christ's love for us. God's sovereign guidance in light of offering us forgiveness from sin is a gift that we must humbly embrace. In embracing this gift, we must then be unapologetic in extending the gift of forgiveness to our neighbors.

God is sovereignly guiding us towards the feet of his Son, Jesus Christ. As we approach the throne of grace in humility, we will understand that we are certainly undeserving of the Lord's forgiveness. This doesn't change the fact that God is running after us in anticipation that we will acknowledge our sin, as we repent and seek him. The hope is that in doing so, we would be a people who seek to offer forgiveness to all. This reality is easier said than done on our own; but with God nothing will be impossible (Luke 1:37, NKJV).

Concluding Thoughts

As we try to pave the way for our lives, we realize that we put matters into our own hands. This gives us a sense to change direction; change our plans; rethink our posture; etc. By making the decision to follow God's sovereign guidance, we surrender our lives, in full submission to him. As we navigate our decisions as Christ followers, we know that no matter what may come our way, God is in control in the midst of this journey called life. There is freedom in this truth. We experience freedom because it is not up to us to control the various details in life. God will pave the way for our steps. God will guide us as we put our trust in him. Regardless of the weight we may carry, God wants to enter into our very lives and set us free from all of our iniquities. He is faithful to meet us in our brokenness and, by his grace, offer us salvation in Christ. Let us take a leap of faith and trust God's sovereign guidance to lead us into his presence.

Questions for Reflection

1. Why is it easier to make your own life plans as opposed to trusting God to guide your steps?

2. What steps of obedience do you need to take in your faith?

3. How do you specifically discern the will of God for your life?

4. How can you fully surrender your trust to God?

Reflections on Chapter 7 | **God's Sovereign Guidance**

"God will guide us as we put our trust in him."

Part Three

New Life

Chapter 8 | A Love We Don't Deserve

*Many are the woes of the wicked, but the Lord's unfailing
love surrounds the one who trusts in him.*

—PSALM 32:10

B etween you and I, this might have been my favorite chapter
to write in the whole book—specifically because I am ob-
sessed with the grace of God. Perhaps you've heard the popular
Christian song "How He Loves,"[1] written by John Mark McMillan.
In that song, there is a verse that continues to play in my head . . .
McMillan writes, "If His grace is an ocean, we're all sinking." Let's
wrap our minds around the meaning of this for a moment. If grace
is an ocean, every single one of us is sinking. Can you picture sinking in the depths of an ocean? In one sense, the thought is scary.
But let's think about this from the angle of God's grace. We are
literally sinking in the grace of God. The abundance of his grace
is endless. It is never-ending. Let's take a moment to pause and let
this truly pierce our minds. We're talking about the love of God
that is offered to us as being immeasurable. We cannot comprehend the depths of his love. We're simply sinking in the goodness,
grace, and love of God.

Unfailing Love

In this verse, David is fully aware of the woes that the wicked portray. In light of this, David's full confidence and assurance is in the

---

1. McMillan, "How He Loves."

Lord's unfailing love—especially to those who trust in the Lord. The reason this specifically works for those who trust in the Lord is because trust expresses our confidence in him. Those who put their utmost confidence in the Lord believe that no matter what comes their way, they can be confident that God is working out all things together for their good. That may not be visible immediately, but God is indeed working in the process of all things. If we believe that, we will see that his love is unfailing towards us. But trusting can be complicated. It can be difficult to trust God in our troubles. We may wonder why a loving God would allow us to experience pain and suffering—among other questions. These are valid questions. The good news still remains. Even if we're questioning, God continues to ruthlessly pursue and love us. Those who trust in his plan will may experience a confidence unlike others. Whether we choose to trust God and his plans for us, he will continue to offer us a love we don't deserve.

But I Am Unworthy . . .

But what if we're not worthy enough, or good enough to receive this love from God? I've spoken with many people who feel this way. In my conversations, people often mention that they feel as though they are too far from God because of personal decisions. They feel like they can't *right their wrongs* and embrace God's love. I remember a particular conversation I had with an individual regarding this feeling of being unworthy. He said to me, "I've done too much wrong in my life to believe that God wants someone like me." He went on, "I'm simply not good enough. I can't have a relationship with a perfect God. There is way too much to fix in my life before I pursue God. I'm not worthy."

Hearing my friend make this statement really hurt me. Mostly because he was struggling to believe who God truly is. Then it dawned on me—I wonder how many people in this world believe the same thing, that they're not ready to pursue a relationship with God because they *aren't good enough*. The truth is that no one is good enough to have a relationship with God. He is perfect and we are not. But God loves us to the degree that he desires to be near to us. He desires to pursue us even though we are unworthy of a relationship with him. This is because God is filled with grace towards humanity and chooses to pursue humanity with love. If one feels unworthy of God's love, we must understand that through the love of Christ we are made worthy. God sent Jesus into this world to mend the brokenness that exists. Although this world is filled with imperfection, Christ is still at work. When we feel unworthy of God's love for us, we need to remember that the gift of Christ has already been sent to us. God's love had been freely given regardless of us feeling unworthy. So yes, it could feel like we don't deserve the love of God because we are indeed unworthy, but that does not mean that he doesn't love us. God's love is displayed through the work of Christ by bringing about our reconciliation to him. There is nothing that we have done for this act of love to transpire. When we feel unworthy, we are welcome at the table of Christ. He desires our presence there. The good news is that our standards of living cannot measure up with God's standards—yet God still overwhelms us with his love. God wants us to know that he welcomes us with open arms to participate in the scandal of grace. Undeserved forgiveness is freely offered to us. It truly is a love we don't deserve.

Loving Others

God's love is something that we don't deserve in our broken and sinful personhood. Regardless, God sent his Son so that we may have the opportunity to respond in faith—receiving and embracing forgiveness and grace. In this, we are set free from our sin and bondage as we are given the privilege to live in Christ, forever, as recipients of God's love. But what does it look like to love and forgive others? How do we understand love regarding those who have hurt us deeply? The reality is that we often desire forgiveness but don't want to offer it to those who have wronged us. Not only that, but when we disagree with someone, our initial inclination may be to dismiss them; remove them from our lives; or to simply ignore them. I'm not saying that we must be friends with everyone, but we can't store up bitterness towards others, holding it against them. Just like we receive a love we don't deserve, we too, must offer a love that others may not deserve.

In Old Testament times, many rules, regulations, and laws existed. When it came to laws that must be followed, the list was endless. In fact, there are 613 different Old Testament commandments.[2] These commands were intended to be obeyed and followed by the Old Testament people.

Jesus arrived, as recorded in the New Testament, not to abolish the law, but to fulfill it (Matt 5:17). No one is capable of following each one of these laws according to their intent. Christ came to be the ultimate fulfillment of the law. During his ministry, Christ was approached by an expert of the law. This expert of the law asked a very important question: "Teacher, which is the greatest commandment in the Law?" (Matt 22:36, NIV). The way Jesus would respond to this question changed everything. The whole approach to the law was summed up in a few profound, life-changing words. Jesus replied, "'Love the Lord your God with all your heart and with all your soul and with all your mind.' This is the first and greatest commandment. And the second is like it: 'Love your neighbor as yourself.' All the Law and the Prophets hang on these two commandments" (Matt 22:37–40, NIV). One commentator helps us understand these commands at a deeper level:

> They remain commandments of God, but they find their coherence in the overriding principle of the double commandment to love. Jesus' words here are not, then, a recommendation of what has come to be known as 'situationalism', the view that there are no principles for Christian conduct other than to do the most loving thing in the given situation. Rather they direct us to understand and apply the commandments of the law within the context of an obligation to love God and man, an

2. Campbell, "Bible Interpretation," 28–29.

obligation of which the commandments are themselves particular expressions.[3]

Jesus has taken the entire Old Testament law and condensed it to what matters most. Love God, love others. Our duty is to love God and to love others well. If we are forgiven by the God of the universe, and we are to bear his image, forgiving and loving others must be at the core of who we are. This is never an easy task, but this is why we must rely on the Spirit of God to give us boldness and courage to forgive and love people.

Forgiveness and love offers a kind of freedom that brings relationships into their initial intent. We were created for one another—for relationship—and due to sin, we have been separated from one another. As believers, we must seek reconciliation with the world as this is the hope of Christ. The apostle Paul makes note of this in his second letter to the Corinthians:

> So from now on we regard no one from a worldly point of view. Though we once regarded Christ in this way, we do so no longer. Therefore, if anyone is in Christ, the new creation has come: The old has gone, the new is here! All this is from God, who reconciled us to himself through Christ and gave us the ministry of reconciliation: that God was reconciling the world to himself in Christ, not counting people's sins against them. And he has committed to us the message of reconciliation. We are therefore Christ's ambassadors, as though God were making his appeal through us. We implore you on Christ's behalf: Be reconciled to God. God made him who had no sin to be sin for us, so that in him we might become the righteousness of God. (2 Cor 5:16–21, NIV)

In Christ, we are a new creation! Praise God for this. Being in Christ also means that we are Christ's ambassadors. The hope is that God would use us as ambassadors in order to bring reconciliation to a broken world. This can only be achieved through the platform of love. Every single person matters to God—which by default should mean that every person that we encounter should

3. France, *Matthew*, 323.

matter to us. Although we may disagree with various lifestyles and preferences, this should not be a reason to disregard the importance of an individual. Just because someone does not fit our mold of the *preferred* individual does not mean that we are to devalue their significance. Every individual is created in the image of God and we are to treat them as such. How much better would this world be if we loved others well? How much more would people engage with the Christian faith if we presented it in love? I believe that by demonstrating a Christlike love towards *all*, many of us would be thoroughly surprised at what God could do in and through us. Love is at the epicenter of reconciliation in this world. Without love, nothing else matters. Each individual longs to be loved. Without love, Christ would not have come into this world to give us hope. Without love, life wouldn't have meaning. Without love, relationships are broken. This is where God's grace comes in. Grace says that you're not worthy of being loved, yet you will be loved all the more. Grace says that when you're not good enough, you still matter; you have a purpose; and you're forgiven. Grace is God in the form of man—Jesus Christ—who willingly steps out of his comfort zone, to bring hope, restoration, and love into a world that is seemingly without hope. Not one single person has ever deserved the love of God through Christ Jesus. But God, in his faithfulness and willingness to love and pursue humanity, offers everyone a love that is undeserved. Due to this, we, too, must seek to offer a love that others may not deserve.

We are active participants in God's unending grace. The more we live in his grace, the more we realize how incredible it is to live in it. God reconciled the world to himself through forgiveness. He chose to forgive the wrongs that were committed against him. Not only that, but he chooses to continuously offer his forgiveness to us. This means that today, by God's grace, we are offered forgiveness. Tomorrow, we will fail God, ourselves, and others, yet in his grace, he will forgive us. This is the beautiful reality of the very character of God. God longs to offer us forgiveness through his Son, Jesus Christ. As followers of Jesus, let us bear God's very image by offering forgiveness towards others. Those who don't deserve it. Those who didn't earn it. Those who continue to fail us, time and time again. Let us offer them love. Let us display God's very character through the way that we conduct ourselves and live. Let us seek the very heart of God, loving him with all of our heart, soul, and mind. Then, let us seek to bring reconciliation into this world by way of love: treating people the way God treats us; offering hope to a world that needs love; offering love to people who need forgiveness; offering forgiveness because forgiveness has been given to us. Rest in his grace.

Questions for Reflection

1. In your understanding, what comes to mind when you think of love?

2. How have you failed to love others well?

3. How does the unending grace of God allow you to take a step of faith, offering love to others?

4. What action steps can you take to offer love towards those who may be unlovable?

5. Who do you need to forgive in your life? How can you pursue reconciliation in that relationship?

Reflections on Chapter 8 | **A Love We Don't Deserve**

"Grace says that you're not worthy of being loved, yet you will be loved all the more."

Chapter 9 | Enjoying God

Rejoice in the Lord and be glad, you righteous;
sing, all you who are upright in heart!

—Psalm 32:11

I find myself to be someone who enjoys a variety of hobbies. I've enjoyed a good bit of coffee roasting, fishing, baseball card collecting, book reading, exercising, and traveling—just to name a few. These things have helped me find enjoyment in a life that is filled with busyness, stress, anxiety, frustration, and the never-ending to-do lists. We all desire to find enjoyable things in our lives. We look to them when we're trying to *spend* our time. But many of our hobbies can only temporarily satisfy us. Because of this, they leave us always wanting more and never fully fill us up. But what if we believed that what we truly desire more of is Christ? What if Jesus was enough for us? This would change everything!

David

David had a crazy life. He made countless mistakes and, often, was self-absorbed. He came to many low points in his journey. But that did not stop him from experiencing the beauty of who God is. God was David's Savior. He was sovereign over his life and provided lots of opportunities for David to be in awe and wonder of all that surrounded him. In the midst of his sins and flaws, David was able to experience the goodness of God. Frequently David would pause and take in the depths of God's character, his creation, and his wonder. Take a look at this wonderful psalm that David put together:

Lord, our Lord,
> how majestic is your name in all the earth!

You have set your glory
> in the heavens.

Through the praise of children and infants
> you have established a stronghold against your enemies,
> to silence the foe and the avenger.

When I consider your heavens,
> the work of your fingers,

the moon and the stars,
> which you have set in place,

what is mankind that you are mindful of them,
> human beings that you care for them?

You have made them a little lower than the angels
> and crowned them with glory and honor.

You made them rulers over the works of your hands;
> you put everything under their feet:

all flocks and herds,
> and the animals of the wild,

the birds in the sky,
> and the fish in the sea,
> all that swim the paths of the seas.

Lord, our Lord,
> how majestic is your name in all the earth!
> (Ps 8:1–9, NIV)

David is in complete awe of God. He emphasizes that God is majestic in all the earth. David is aware of God's hand at work in all of creation and he writes this psalm as a response. One commentator helps us understand the depth of Psalm 8:

> This psalm is an unsurpassed example of what a hymn should be, celebrating as it does the glory and grace of God, rehearsing who he is and what he has done, and relating us and our world to him; all with a masterly economy of words, and in a spirit of mingled joy and awe. It brings to light the unexpectedness of God's ways in the roles he has assigned to the strong and the weak (2), the spectacular and the obscure (3–5), the multitudinous and the few (6–8); but it begins and ends with God himself, and its overriding theme is 'How excellent is thy name!'[1]

Kidner helps us understand that this psalm celebrates the glory and grace of God. God's grace is an incredible benefit to all who exist. He bestows his grace upon us in a variety of ways. David experiences and enjoys the grace of God through declaring that God has set his glory in the heavens. David is fully aware of God's handiwork among the moon and the stars as he is mesmerized by it. In light of the depths of who God is, David asks, "What is mankind that you are mindful of them?" (Psalm 8:4, NIV). We need to understand this before moving forward: God is the Creator of the universe—and everything that is in it—and yet he is mindful of mankind. This is because God desires to have a personal relationship with all people. He created mankind for his enjoyment and desires that we may enjoy him and one another.

How often do we take a pause and reflect on God's goodness and creation? Everything that is seen and unseen God authored for our enjoyment. His desire is that we do not take for granted the handiwork of his creativity. We are given the opportunity to experience the grace of God towards us as we absorb the breathtaking beauty that is among us.

Reflection

Reflection is another way that we can enjoy God and his goodness. Each day we have a list of "to-do's" that we need to take care of. We have obligations and responsibilities, which always keep us on the

1. Kidner, *Psalms 1–72*, 82.

go. Living like this can pull us from the discipline of reflection. What if we were to pause for a moment and realize that the Lord—in his grace—had given us breath in our lungs today? Praise God! His grace is being extended to us in the midst of our breath. Take a moment to take this in and reflect on the goodness of God.

Reflection allows us to process and comprehend. When we reflect on God's work throughout the history of the world, we're able to see his faithfulness to his people. Countless times, he has made promises, which he fulfilled. The Bible is filled with many of God's promises to his people, but the one that stands out most is in the story of Abraham. In Genesis, God made a promise to Abram:

> The Lord had said to Abram, "Go from your country, your people and your father's household to the land I will show you.
>
>> "I will make you into a great nation,
>>   and I will bless you;
>> I will make your name great,
>>   and you will be a blessing.
>> I will bless those who bless you,
>>   and whoever curses you I will curse;
>> and all peoples on earth
>>   will be blessed through you." (Gen 12:1–3, NIV)

This call required complete faith and trust in God's plan. God was calling Abram to abandon his country, his people, and his father's household so that he could give him a land. In Abram's obedience, he would be made into a great nation and experience the many blessings that God would grant him. All peoples on earth would be blessed by Abram's obedience. Did God follow through on this promise? Paul answers this question in his letter to the Galatians:

> Brothers and sisters, let me take an example from everyday life. Just as no one can set aside or add to a human covenant that has been duly established, so it is in this case. The promises were spoken to Abraham and to his seed. Scripture does not say "and to seeds," meaning many people, but "and to your seed," meaning one person, who is Christ. What I mean is this: The law, introduced 430

years later, does not set aside the covenant previously established by God and thus do away with the promise. For if the inheritance depends on the law, then it no longer depends on the promise; but God in his grace gave it to Abraham through a promise. (Gal 3:15–18)

God is faithful in his promises to humanity. Paul affirmed and confirmed God's promise to Abraham. Paul specifically uses the language of "God in his grace." God made a promise to Abram back in Genesis and that promise was fulfilled by the grace of God. He is faithful. We can reflect on the faithfulness of who God is throughout the history of the world. God is who he says he is. He comes through when he makes a promise. This is found all over Scripture. We, too, can experience the promises of God—namely, in the work of the gospel. He offers us his faithful grace by sending us his Son, Jesus Christ. Let us reflect on this earnest gift from above. God is filled with grace towards us even though we are unworthy of it. Take a moment and reflect on this beautiful mystery. This is a way for us to enjoy our personal Creator.

Relationships

As mentioned earlier, God created us for relationships. He is a personal being. From the very beginning—at the garden of Eden—God engaged in conversation. God spoke all things into existence and then he created mankind. Once mankind was created, God spoke to Adam and Eve because he wanted to be in relationship with them. We talked in chapter 2 about the law that God gave to Moses in Exodus. This was God speaking to Moses because God wanted to be direct and personal. God spoke to David as he made him a promise (2 Sam 7).

We see God's personhood revealed in the form of Jesus Christ, who is God in the flesh. God incarnated himself so that he could be among us—living the very life that we live. He did this so that he could experience all things that we experience, yet he was perfect and knew no sin (2 Cor 5:21). God became incarnate so that he could participate in the human experience, in his perfection, so that he could forgive the sins of all, giving us hope and life eternal. He did this because he loves us (John 3:16–17). God yearns for human relationships because he loves us. He longs to restore us back to himself through Christ. He meets us where we're at, understands our stories, and longs to dwell among us by way of the Holy Spirit. The Holy Spirit is given to all who believe in Christ Jesus as their Lord and Savior as a seal of our salvation (Eph 1:13). We participate in our relationship with God through the power of the Holy Spirit so that we may become like Christ. God has given us the Spirit as a reminder that he is with us—always. Let us rejoice and be glad that our God longs for us. Our sin is forgiven and our transgressions are wiped away! We are made new in Christ Jesus and participate in an eternal relationship with him. We become a new creation in Christ. "Therefore, if anyone is in Christ, the new creation has come: The old has gone, the new is here!" (2 Cor 5:17, NIV). Commentator Colin G. Kruse states:

> The thrust of this statement is that when a person is *in Christ*, he or she is part of the new creation. God's plan of salvation, while primarily concerned with humanity, encompasses the whole created order (Rom. 8:21). When a person is *in Christ* he or she has become already part of the new creation so that it may be said, *the old has passed away, behold, the new has come.*[2]

God is working on restoring all things. This includes creation as well as humanity. He wants to restore our relationship with him. He wants to restore our relationships with others. He wants to restore our suffering; our hurt; our addictions; our fears; our frustrations; our pain; and our story. The work of the cross has already taken place. Let us live in Christ and desire to be made one with him. Let us long to enjoy our Creator and our Savior. The moment we find absolute joy and satisfaction in our Savior is the moment our lives will change forever. By the grace of God, we are forgiven.

---

2. Kruse, *2 Corinthians*, 124.

Questions for Reflection

1. Would you say that you're constantly on the go, not having time to pause and reflect? Why or why not?

2. How can you intentionally pursue authentic reflection on the goodness of God?

3. What are some things that you can reflect on and absorb to their fullest?

4. How can the posture of reflection change who you are as a person?

5. What can you omit from your life that could allow you to reflect more?

Reflections on Chapter 9 | **Enjoying God**

"Everything that is seen and unseen
God authored for our enjoyment."

Wrapping It Up

Through the living testimony of a forgiven sinner, David illustrated the power of God's grace and forgiveness to all who would humble themselves in receiving this forgiveness. He knew that God was a God of unending forgiveness, infinite grace, reckless love, giver of second-chances, redeemer of all sin. He trusted in these truths about God. David knew that when he had wronged God, he needed to repent of his sin, changing his behavior and actions. He knew that apart from God's help, this was an impossible act to achieve. Regardless of David's flaws, it was only by the grace of God that he could receive assurance that he was indeed forgiven—regardless of the sin. David knew that the God he served was gracious and loving, but it would take a crucial step of obedience on his part in order for him to experience and understand these profound gifts of God.

My dear friends, we join together as a community of sinners in need of a Savior. This Savior has demonstrated his faithful love towards us by entering into our very nature and being. In doing so, he experienced anger, pain, hurt, sorrow, temptation, yet without sin—something none of us could accomplish. In order for us to be made right with God, we need to present ourselves as perfect beings before a holy God. This of course is unattainable. Therefore Christ Jesus set foot into our context, living a perfect life on our behalf while giving himself up to the point of death on the cross at Calvary. He gave his life up for us so that we might be forgiven from our sin and live in harmony with God the Father Almighty.

Each one of us is welcome to participate in this profound narrative of hope and restoration. We have the choice to commit ourselves to following Christ for the duration of our lives and into eternity. The key is that we recognize that we cannot carry

ourselves on our own. We are in desperate need of grace and a
mercy. Praise be to God for giving us a love we don't deserve—a
love so beautiful that we can enter into God's forgiveness through
his wonderful grace. So let us go in peace as we continue to discover and embrace the love of Christ, who is for us, while offering
this same love towards others.

Biblical Texts for Further Study on Grace

The Word became flesh and made his dwelling among us. We have seen his glory, the glory of the one and only Son, who came from the Father, full of grace and truth.

—JOHN 1:14

For sin shall no longer be your master, because you are not under the law, but under grace.

—ROMANS 6:14

And if by grace, then it cannot be based on works; if it were, grace would no longer be grace.

—ROMANS 11:6

For it is by grace you have been saved, through faith—and this is not from yourselves, it is the gift of God—not by works, so that no one can boast.

—EPHESIANS 2:8–9

For the grace of God has appeared that offers salvation to all people.

—TITUS 2:11

Let us then approach God's throne of grace with confidence, so that we may receive mercy and find grace to help us in our time of need.

—HEBREWS 4:16

Biblical Texts for Further Study on Forgiveness

For if you forgive other people when they sin against you, your heavenly Father will also forgive you. But if you do not forgive others their sins, your Father will not forgive your sins.

—MATTHEW 6:14–15

"So watch yourselves. If your brother or sister sins against you, rebuke them; and if they repent, forgive them. Even if they sin against you seven times in a day and seven times come back to you saying 'I repent,' you must forgive them."

—LUKE 17:3–4

Get rid of all bitterness, rage and anger, brawling and slander, along with every form of malice. Be kind and compassionate to one another, forgiving each other, just as in Christ God forgave you.

—EPHESIANS 4:31–32

Bear with each other and forgive one another if any of you has a grievance against someone. Forgive as the Lord forgave you.

—COLOSSIANS 3:13

If we confess our sins, he is faithful and just and will forgive us our sins and purify us from all unrighteousness.

—1 JOHN 1:9

Bibliography

Allen, Leslie C. "Romans." New International Bible Commentary. Edited by F. F. Bruce. Zondervan, 1986.

Bonhoeffer, Dietrich. *Ethics*. New York: Touchstone, 1995.

Bruce, F. F. *The Epistle to the Hebrews*. Grand Rapids: Eerdmans, 2018.

Calvin, John. *Institutes of the Christian Religion*. Rev. ed. Peabody, MA: Hendrickson, 2007.

Campbell, D. K. "Bible Interpretation—Then and Now." In *Basic Bible Interpretation: A Practical Guide to Discovering Biblical Truth*, by Roy B. Zuck, edited by C. Bubeck Sr., 28–29. Colorado Springs: David C. Cook, 1991.

Erickson, Millard J. *Christian Theology*. 3rd edition. Grand Rapids: Baker Academic, 2013.

France, R. T. *Matthew: An Introduction and Commentary*. Tyndale New Testament Commentaries 1. Downers Grove: InterVarsity, 1985.

Ingram, Chip. *The Real God: How He Longs for You to See Him*. Grand Rapids: Baker, 2016.

Keller, Tim. *The Prodigal God: Recovering the Heart of the Christian Faith*. New York: Penguin, 2008.

Kidner, Derek. *Psalms 1–72: An Introduction and Commentary*. Tyndale Old Testament Commentaries 15. Downers Grove: InterVarsity, 1973.

Kruse, Colin G. *2 Corinthians: An Introduction and Commentary*. Tyndale New Testament Commentaries 8. Downers Grove: InterVarsity, 1987.

McMillan, John Mark. "How He Loves." Integrity Music, 2010.

Spurgeon, Charles H. *The Complete Works of C. H. Spurgeon*. Vol. 14, "Sermons 788 to 847." Fort Collins, CO: Delmarva, 2015.

Wambsgans, E. Jason. "Abandoned on LSD." Photo in "From the Archives: The Blizzard of 2011." *Chicago Tribune*. https://www.chicagotribune.com/weather/chi-110201-monster-snowstorm-2011-pictures-photogallery.html.

Author Index

Subject Index

Scripture Index